MW00901978

A
FOSTER KID'S
ROAD TO
SUCCESS

A
FOSTER KID'S
ROAD TO
SUCCESS

ROBERT P.K. MOONEY

A Foster Kid's Road to Success
Copyright © 2020 by Robert P.K. Mooney

All rights reserved. No part of this publication may be reproduced or transmitted in any form or by any means electronic or mechanical, including photocopy, recording, or any information storage and retrieval system now known or to be invented, without permission in writing from the publisher, except by a reviewer who wishes to quote brief passages in connection with a review written for inclusion in a magazine, newspaper, website, or broadcast.

Published in the United States by
RPKM Publishing, LLC
877 East 1200 South
#970531
Orem, Utah 84097

Book Cover Design: Amier WildEagle
Book Interior Design: Francine Eden Platt • Eden Graphics, Inc.

Library of Congress Control Number: Pending

978-1-7347969-0-2 Paperback
978-1-7347969-1-9 ePub

Printed in the United States of America

10 9 8 7 6 5 4 3 2 1

Dedication:

To NICKBO—you give meaning to everything that I do.

To Kim—thanks for not voting me out of the house before I ever got there.

To Mom and Dad—thanks for not voting me out of the house after I got there and helping an older foster kid grow into a man, husband and father.

Finally, **to Michelle and Kurt**—you are still loved and still missed. Every. Single. Day.

TABLE OF CONTENTS

ACKNOWLEDGMENTS

This work would not have been possible but for the insight, input and support of countless individuals—far too many to name. But there are a few who I feel I need to give a specific shoutout to.

I am indebted to each of the many foster and adoptive parents who opened their homes to me and my siblings over the course of more than a decade. Thank you for your sacrifice and service. I am especially grateful for Susan, who braved trying to corral a 9-year-old foster kid as a single parent, and who has sheltered me with her love for over thirty years after I left her physical care.

I am grateful for all of my professional colleagues who encouraged me to write a book. Even though this isn't really the book they urged me to write—a detailed memoir of my journey as a foster kid—I hope this book directed at inspiring teens in foster care will serve a far better purpose.

There is no way that this book would have become a reality without the mentorship and guidance of Richard Paul Evans. His knowledge and experience, which he was so generous in sharing, were critical to getting *A Foster Kid's Road To Success* written and edited, its cover designed, and then finally published and distributed.

I'd like to thank my editor, the amazing Sydny Miner. Her thoughtful input, insights and suggestions were critical to taking this manuscript from a rough cut to a book I could share with the world.

I am especially grateful for my research assistant, Isaac, who spent hours upon hours compiling the practical resources contained in the Appendix of this book, which point older teens in foster care to various sources of educational, housing and healthcare assistance.

Thank you to my beautiful wife and children. They endured fifteen years of long hours and prolonged absences while I was a lawyer, only to have to endure long hours (but less absences) with me writing and rewriting this book and others to follow. Thank you for your love and support!

Finally, my sincere gratitude goes to my Father in Heaven, whose Divine Providence has been in my life from the beginning, even before I knew He was there, and even when I couldn't feel His presence. He has healed what could not be healed and fixed those things that were broken beyond repair.

PREFACE

When you're a foster kid, it can feel like the deck is stacked against you.

I know. I spent the last twelve years of my childhood as a foster kid, changing homes, on average, every seven months—a total of twenty moves. I did not have biological parents willing and able to nurture and care for me and to put my needs above theirs. Like you, I've experienced hurt, loneliness, abuse, rejection, and abandonment. Maybe worst of all, I've felt the pain of separation. Separation from parents, brothers, and sisters. Separation from a home you had hoped would be the last.

I know what it feels like to close your eyes, put your head down on your desk at school and wish, "When I open my eyes, this will all have been just a dream and I'll be home." I know what it is like to have feelings of love interlaced with fear and hatred, and a seemingly unquenchable yearning for connection with those who hurt me most. I carry those scars, and I know you do too, if not on the outside, then certainly on the inside.

Under the circumstances, it isn't surprising if you feel like you want to take the easy way and give up. Why not? Why should you care about what happens to you if no one else does? Because I care, and I expect more of you.

You see, while you and I have something in common, I know something you may not. You are *needed*. Too many kids do not understand how to do hard things. They don't know how to stand back up after getting knocked down. They don't know how to endure. Because of your experiences as a foster kid, you are someone who has, from an early age, had to face unspeakable challenges. You have had to find a way to survive, persevere, endure, and overcome pain, heartache and loss.

That ability to overcome is needed in the world today. You are needed to be an example—an example to your classmates, to your co-workers, and to others in your community. By choosing to be successful, you can live a life full of meaning, love, and belonging. And when you choose to be successful, even with all that you have been through, others will realize that they can choose to be successful too. I want to show you how.

Although this book is not, strictly speaking, a memoir of my life, I share a number of stories from my years as a foster kid and beyond. So, a brief biographical sketch about me may be helpful as I refer to stories from my childhood.

I was born in Honolulu, Hawaii in 1978. My biological

parents each had been married before they got together, and each had two living children from their first marriages. I was the third of seven children born to their union.

I look relatively racially ambiguous, with olive skin, dark brown hair, and dark brown eyes. When people hear that I was born in Hawaii, they frequently assume that I am Polynesian. Others, who don't know where I was born, have asked if I am Hispanic, Italian, or part Eastern Asian. My darker complexion, however, comes from my biological father's Native American heritage. He grew up believing that he was Cherokee, but later found that his principal Native American tribal heritage was Seminole. My mother, on the other hand, was exceptionally fair with red hair and green eyes from her Scandinavian heritage. I have the darkest natural complexion of my siblings, and in the Hawaiian sun, I get extremely dark-skinned.

When I was six years old, my six full biological siblings and I (my half-siblings were adults and living on their own) were placed into custody of the State of Hawaii. In order to distinguish between my biological parents and any foster parents discussed in this book, I'll generally refer to my biological parents as my "father" or "mother," and any foster parents as a "foster dad" or "foster mom" as the case may be. Similarly, I'll refer to my biological siblings simply as my "siblings," or my "brother[s]" or "sister[s]." Foster siblings will be designated as such.

In Hawaii, I changed foster homes six times. On my eighth birthday, I moved from Oahu to Provo, Utah. My mother was dying of cancer—non-Hodgkin's lymphoma—and she requested that Hawaii State officials relocate me and my siblings to Utah where her parents and siblings lived, and where she had moved some time after me and my siblings went into foster care.

In Utah, I changed homes another fourteen times, with my last foster home change coming the summer before my senior year in high school. Although I aged out of the system without being adopted, my last foster family has become, over time, the one that I call my own, and whom my children consider their "grandma," "grandpa," and extended family.

After high school, I went to college and got a bachelor's degree in business. In my senior year of college, I married a woman I met during my high school years and reconnected with during my junior year of college.

After a short period of full-time work following graduation, I returned to school for a law degree. After law school graduation, I began practicing law as a business trial lawyer. In 2019, I stepped away from my legal practice to write this book, and to speak to groups of older foster kids throughout the country, sharing the principles taught in this book. My hope is to inspire kids likely to age out of foster care to rise above what the statistics suggest they are likely destined to become.

Those statistics are grim. They indicate that one in five foster kids in the United States that age out of the system become instantly homeless, and only 50% of the youth who age out are able to receive some sort of employment by the time they are 24 years old. Only 3% of foster kids who age out graduate from college.

Rather than become one of those statistics, I chose to model the best of what I saw in my many foster homes and not the worst that I experienced in my childhood. I chose to create and protect a family. I chose to not be a foster-care statistic. I want to help you choose to do the same.

You see, you are not a statistic to me. You are unique, and you are special, and your story will be your own. What do you want to accomplish in this life? What do you want to become? Who do you aspire to be? In this book, I'll show you how to choose *your* path to success. I'll tell you how I found a way to get past the pain and loneliness, and how I discovered to be part of a family with meaningful and enduring relationships. I'll share the principles and the path that led a beaten and broken kid to forge fulfilling emotional relationships and a successful life. I did it, and you can do it too.

---- CHAPTER 1 ----

KNOW THAT YOU CAN

There are thousands of books about self-improvement. They all claim to lead to some specified desired end: knowledge, wealth, fitness, friendship, self-control, happiness. Before any of those guides can help you, the first thing you must understand is this one truth: only you have the power to do it.

What is "it," you ask? *Anything.* You can do anything—even things that the world tells you that you can't.

When I was five years old, I saw thousands of people jogging near my home in Oahu. I asked my father, "What are all these people running from?" He responded, "It's the Honolulu Marathon."

That didn't answer my question—I had no idea what a marathon was. So, I pressed. "What is a marathon?"

"It's a 26-mile race," he replied.

You know what my response was? Unabashed, naïve confidence. I looked up at him, and with a completely straight face, told him, "I can do that." And I believed it. At that point, I had no reason to believe that I *couldn't* do it. At five years old, I had no clue what running a marathon really meant, or what it required, and I had no concept of how far 26 miles was. All I knew was that I wanted to do it. Also, I had seen Sylvester Stallone's *Rocky* with its unforgettable training montage, so I figured that I would have to do some sort of training.

I convinced my older brother, who was seven, and my older sister, who was nine, that they should run with me during the next annual marathon—twelve months away. My sister was instantly on board. My brother was a harder sell. At first, he told me I was stupid, but when he realized I was going to do it anyway, he wasn't going to be shown up by his little brother. He was in.

Our training regime was about as complex as you'd expect from little kids. We did push-ups, sit-ups, and of course, we ran. The three of us ran up and down a hill near our home. It was about a three-mile round trip. I got it in my head that we should sprint the last 100 yards, so that's what we did. I always lost. Every day—up the hill, down the hill. Up the hill, down the hill. It turns out that relying exclusively on a daily three-mile jog with a 100-yard sprint is no way to train for a marathon! But I didn't know that.

Our father was a casual jogger, and he seemed to think it cute that his children thought they could run a marathon. He started jogging with us, but it wasn't long before he dropped out and forgot all about the race. Sometimes my mother would drive her station wagon beside us as we ran, but significant health issues frequently kept her in bed. Sometimes my brother and sister didn't feel like training, so I would go it alone.

A few months later, we moved from that house to an apartment. With the marathon still many months away, I knew that we still needed to train, so we made a new route.

In September, three months before the marathon, I turned six. My mother signed me, my brother, my sister, and my father up for the race.

For a six-year-old, a year's worth of training seemed nearly a lifetime. But eventually, December came, and with it came the race day. The afternoon before the marathon, my mother left the house and didn't return for hours—well after nightfall. I was terrified. This was not normal for my mother, as she was almost always home when it was time for me to go to bed. The race started at 5:00 a.m. and I should have been sleeping, but I was worried about my mother. She came home at around 10:00 p.m. The cause for her late night? She had made t-shirts that said "Mooney Bunch" for us and had purchased matching red running shorts with white stripes up the side, and matching tube socks with red rings on the top. It wasn't until my mother returned with our matching outfits that my father remembered that he had agreed to run the race with us.

We were all awake hours before sunrise to get ready. Apart from the outfits my mother had purchased the night before, we did not have any running gear to speak of. Marathoners these days run their races with scientifically designed running shoes and high-tech devices to measure, report and track the runner's distance, pace and heart rate. They run with hydration belts where they carry electrolyte-filled water bottles and sweetened chews or gels to help give them energy to last through the 26-mile ordeal. We didn't have any of that. Rather, all I was equipped with was a pair of worn out, thin-soled grey sneakers. They didn't even have laces—they were the two Velcro-strap variety!

Once we were suited up, we drove towards downtown Honolulu, but had to park far away from the start of the race because of the crowds. We hitchhiked a ride to the starting line and joined the thousands of runners—all of whom towered over me—waiting for the race to begin.

With a bang of a gun, the mass of people began to move forward. Within a quarter of a mile, the crowd began to thin out as the faster, more experienced runners separated from the slower ones. I had to take nearly two strides for every one of my father's, but I kept up. It didn't take too long before we reached the three-mile marker—the standard running distance to which I had become accustomed. Three miles turned into five miles turned into ten miles. I just kept going.

Eventually my older brother and sister outpaced me and pulled ahead, but my father slowed his pace to stay with me. Ten miles bled into twelve, then thirteen, fourteen, fifteen miles. I could feel a pain in my toothpick-thin legs unlike any I had ever felt before, but I kept going. I was running slower and slower with every mile, but still running.

At about mile twenty, my legs told my body what my head wouldn't: "Kid, you are done!" My legs seized up and I crashed to the asphalt. I was in excruciating pain from prolonged involuntary and intense hamstring and quadricep contractions that made it impossible for me to extend or bend my legs on my own.

My father sat down next to me, pulled me onto his lap, and rubbed out my legs for twenty minutes. He kneaded the seized, knotted muscles while bending and extending my legs back and forth until the cramps released and I could move my legs again.

By that time, the race officials had opened up parts of the roads to let traffic through. A couple of guys in a rusty tan pickup truck saw me and my father, pulled over and asked if we needed a ride. My father stood up, looked down at me and said, "It's your choice, but you've done a great job. Let's go home."

Twenty miles isn't bad for any six-year-old, especially one who had only ever run three miles at a time. But I did not start the race just to run in it. I started with the intent to make it to the end. I responded, "No thanks, I think I'll finish." Without another word, I stood up on my trembling legs and started running again.

About an hour and a half later, I saw the finish line and I started sprinting, just like I always did on my practice runs. I left my father behind. He only caught up when I was slowed slightly by a couple of spectators who ran up to me during my finishing sprint to place flowered leis around my neck as I ran.

Crossing the finish line of the Honolulu Marathon

After I crossed the finish line, I drew a crowd. I genuinely did not understand what the fuss was about. It seemed that nobody expected a little kid to finish a race of that length—except maybe that little kid. I had no reason to believe that I couldn't do it. I am sure that in the year leading up to the race, there were those who told me that a kid as small and as young as I was couldn't finish a race that long. However, I promptly ignored those people, and their doubts never made it to race day. From the start of the race, until the end, I believed that I could do it. And I did. I was the youngest person to ever finish that race.

I'm telling you this story to help you understand that you can do whatever *your* "it" is. It does not matter if others don't believe you can do it. It does not matter if the statistics are stacked against you. It doesn't matter if other people have tried and failed. They are not you. You can do it.

Something you may have missed in this story: I didn't get to the finish line alone. In fact, it would not have been possible to do it without my father. On the whole, he was not a good parent. Rather, he was selfish, neglectful, and abusive. Notwithstanding his flaws, during the race, he stayed with me as I tried to accomplish what must have appeared to be a foolish goal. When I fell, and was in immense pain, he held me. He rubbed my legs until the pain went away.

In your quest to do whatever it is you set out to do, there will be people along the way who will be there to help. You will fall. You will scrape up your knees from time to time. But there will be others around to help you get back up and keep going. They will be flawed, just like you, but you will find that you don't have to do it all on your own.

While there are countless worthy goals that can be your "it," and I expect that you have many dreams that you hope to achieve, my greatest hope for you is that you know that you can have lasting, meaningful, and intensely fulfilling personal relationships. Having had a successful career filled with accolades, wealth, and amazing travel experiences, I can honestly say that, for me, nothing has been more satisfying than deep and meaningful connections with other people.

I hope, that in all of your achieving, you seek to cultivate and maintain lasting human relationships where you can love and be loved. Trust and be trusted. Know and be known. Growing up as a foster kid, you likely were deprived of those types of relationships in large measure. It is so hard to trust parents who abuse or neglect you. It's hard to let yourself be truly known by a family that is temporary. I get that. But I am here to tell you that those are the types of relationships that will bring you true joy and happiness. I hope you make it your goal to create, protect and maintain healthy interpersonal relationships.

It was only two months after the marathon that my siblings and I were placed into foster care through Hawaii's

Child Welfare Services. The police received a report of domestic violence at our apartment. I never found out for certain who called the police, but I have been told that it was a family member, possibly an older sibling. When the officers knocked at the door, neither of my parents were home. The uniformed men helped us each pack a paper grocery bag with our clothes, and two police cruisers drove us to a battered women and children's shelter, where we met with a social worker.

I don't recall where my mother was when the police came, but by the end of the day, the police had contacted her and convinced her to join me and my siblings at the shelter. I say "convinced," because my mother, like many other domestic abuse victims, found it difficult to flee her abuser. In fact, about six months before the police came, my mother had arranged to fly my siblings and me to the mainland. Her oldest daughter, my half-sister, who was already in college in Utah, flew to Hawaii to pick us up to go live with my mother's sister. However, within two weeks, my father convinced my mother to bring us back to Hawaii, and the abuse and neglect continued.

This time, my mother was persuaded that she and her children needed to get away from my father. However, during our stay at the shelter, it became clear to the social workers that my mother was too ill—physically and mentally—to care for seven young children. Believing it was in our best interest, state officials took me and my siblings into custody and arranged to place us in foster homes.

My first placement was with my best friend's family who lived up the street from our apartment. They immediately signed up to take me in when they discovered I would be placed in foster care.

Unfortunately, that was only temporary while social workers looked for a home that would take all of my siblings. After only a few weeks, our assigned social worker found a foster home that was willing to take a sibling group of seven kids. A case worker picked me up from my friend's house and took me to a hospital where my siblings and I all received vaccinations and other preventative medical care.

My older sister, who was ten at the time, ran away from the hospital. When the police caught up with her, our case worker decided that she should be placed in a home on her own. Two days later, my older brother, who was eight, ran away from the new placement. I remained with my four younger siblings, ages five to one. After a few months, the foster family decided that we were too much to handle, and we were split up and moved. And so began what would be twelve years in the foster system across two states—Hawaii and Utah. After that, the largest group of siblings in any one home was my three youngest. Sometimes I was placed with one of my siblings, but in most placements, I was the only one of my siblings in the home.

For years, I bounced from home to home until being a foster kid became my new normal. Foster care was no longer some event or interruption in life—it *was* my life. No permanency, no roots, no place to call my own.

After my nineteenth home change I realized that I was likely going to age out of the foster care system. I had been in foster care well over half of my life—nine years out of the fifteen I had been alive. By then, my four younger siblings had been adopted by three different families, but I was keenly aware that older teenagers in foster care were not likely to find a permanent home.

At the time, I was living with a friend's family, who had generously agreed to help me escape the very toxic environment that was my previous living situation. Although my friend's family were amazing people, I felt like an outsider and incomplete. I realized that what I was missing was a family that I could call my own. I loved my siblings, but I only saw them upon occasion, as each of them had their own lives separate and apart from the dysfunctional and abusive reality we had shared together years before while living with our biological parents. My older sister had aged out, and was struggling with severe physical and mental illnesses related to our traumatic childhood. My older brother—then seventeen—was living essentially on his own about three hundred miles away. My two younger brothers had been adopted by two different families in Utah, and my two younger sisters had been adopted together.

I realized then that it was likely that I would be responsible for making my own family as an adult. I was assigned a new social worker in Utah, Jayne Carlton. Upon getting my case, Jayne immediately began to help me prepare to transition to adult living. She emphasized the need for me to get an education beyond high school. It's a good thing she did, because in college, I became reacquainted with a young woman, a classmate at my second high school (I changed high schools each year as I changed foster placements). Our first interaction, nearly seven years after we last attended school together went like this:

> Attractive Blonde Girl: "Hey, didn't you go to Mountain View?"
>
> Clueless College Boy: "Yeah, I did."
>
> Attractive Blonde Girl: "And didn't you play basketball?"
>
> Interested College Boy: "Yeah, I did."
>
> Attractive Blonde Girl: "Weren't you that foster kid?"
>
> Smitten College Boy: *Who are you?*"

Great, I was known as "that foster kid." Well, at least she remembered me, and that was certainly worth something! We dated, and although she was a stunningly beautiful young woman, what was most attractive to me was her desire for, and preparation to have, a family. She wanted children, and she deeply wanted to be an amazing mother to those children. She literally went to school for it. Her college major was Marriage, Family and Human Development. When she graduated, she told people that she was "a professional mom with no experience." You can imagine how I would be drawn to a woman who was interested in studying, creating, and maintaining lasting family relationships.

While she seemed like an ideal partner, I was lacking in a number of critical family areas given my turbulent childhood. In fact, I was once told that my future wife would be taking a terrible risk in marrying me. And that was true—I was a risky proposition. How so? Her education gave her some insights to kids with a background similar to mine. Her textbooks told her that over one third of children who are abused as children grow up to become abusers themselves. The risk is even higher when the abuse started early, the abuse lasted for a long time, and the abuser had a close relationship to the child. These all described me. Starting quite young, I had been abused physically, emotionally and sexually within my home. The abuse lasted for years.

And then there was my biological father. While my wife and I were dating, my father was arrested and charged with multiple drug-related offenses. She was afraid of him and fearful of what his involvement with her future children would be.

Notwithstanding all of that, over time, she was able to see beyond my troubled past and recognize that I was determined to not repeat my childhood trauma. Thankfully, she agreed to marry me. We have five children together.

After my first son was born, I received a law degree and started my career at a large law firm. Our next three children joined our family as I struggled to balance my desire to ensure that my wife and children had their physical needs met with my longing to be with them as much as possible. Our fifth child joined our family while I was writing this book—a beautiful bi-racial little girl who would have been placed in foster care at birth but for her adoption into our family.

Our little family unit is the greatest source of belonging and happiness in my life. When we are apart, my soul yearns to be with them.

I felt that yearning most deeply about ten years into my legal career, when I attended a prestigious university to obtain a second law degree. My coursework required me to spend about six weeks in Madrid, Spain with my classmates. Spain! Culture, breathtaking architecture, beautiful people, incredible food! Madrid is absolutely stunning with an amazing history. My studies were difficult but engaging and stimulating. My classmates were accomplished lawyers from around the world. Being there was an incomparable experience.

However, during the long weeks I spent away from my wife and children, I found that my heart ached deeply to be with them. Speaking with and seeing them over video calls was wonderful, but altogether insufficient. I missed holding them in my arms. I missed dancing with my daughter, wrestling with my sons, and kissing their foreheads while they slept in bed when I got home from work after bedtime. I missed lying next to my wife discussing both the meaningless, mundane details of daily tasks, and the more important, memorable moments of life as they occurred. Although I was in a beautiful country and a magnificent city, I was separated from what brought me the deepest joy—my wife and children whose happiness I wanted far more than my own personal comfort. I wanted to be with them, and they wanted to be with me. I needed them, and they needed me.

And so it is today. As of the date of the publication of this book, I have been married for almost twenty years. My children are growing, with my oldest spreading his wings in young adulthood. I want to be with them, and they tell me they want to be with me. I love and I am loved. And those family bonds are the most fulfilling things in my life.

Why tell you about my current family life? Because, while there are hundreds of worthy goals that can be your "it," my greatest hope for you is that you have lasting and intensely fulfilling personal relationships. I've had a successful career filled with accolades, financial security, and amazing travel experiences (work responsibilities have taken me all across the United States and to countries as diverse as

New Zealand, Ireland and Slovenia). After all that, I can tell you that *nothing* is more satisfying or brings more happiness than deep and meaningful relationships with other people.

My hope for you is that you come to know that you can have deep, enduring, nurturing, and fulfilling family connections—all those things that you likely were deprived of while growing up as a foster kid. Know that you can have it. By your very existence, you deserve it. Nothing that has happened to you, nothing that has been done to you, and nothing that you have done forfeits your ability to have profound, mutual human connection.

My friend, you can do amazing things. You can be a productive member of whatever society you choose to be part of. But mostly, I want you to know that you can love and be loved. You just need to know that you can.

CHAPTER 2

YOUR GREATEST TOOL: THE ABILITY TO CHOOSE

You came into this world with one ability that is far greater than any skill, talent, or attribute: the power of choice. As soon as you realize that you have the ability to choose your actions and your response to others' actions, you will quickly realize that *you* are the master of your own fate. It took me a while to realize that I was not merely a product of all the crap that had happened to me as a kid. I reacted to situations, and more often than not, I just did what felt right (but was frequently wrong); I merely acted on instinct.

As I mentioned in the introduction, my first foster home was a temporary placement with my best friend's family. After a few weeks, our case worker found a home willing to take me and all of my siblings—seven kids aged ten and under! Within two days, my ten-year-old sister and eight-year-old brother had separately ran away, were found by the police, and then placed in separate homes. So, it was just me—a six-year-old—and my four younger brothers and sisters in a foreign environment. A strange new home with unfamiliar adults as parents. I was terrified, but notwithstanding my fear, I was determined to protect my younger siblings. I mistrusted my new foster parents, as I viewed them as being complicit to the events that had taken me away from my mother.

I moved to a new elementary school. I was one of the smaller kids in my class and a particularly large boy at the school decided to pick on me. One day he approached me in the hall and took a swing at me. I happened to have a yellow #2 pencil in my left hand. When his fist came at me I leaned back out of his way, and once his arm crossed his body, I stabbed him in the back with the pencil. I know I was disciplined somewhat by the school administration, but frankly, it was not nearly as harsh as one might expect to receive for *stabbing* a schoolmate.

Perhaps the principal was lenient on me, recognizing that I was just defending myself against a much larger aggressor. Some might say that stabbing a bully in the back was excusable, maybe even justified, under the circumstances. In fact, some would applaud the courage and audacity of such a small kid fighting back.

But guess what? It wasn't courage. It was a reaction—not a conscious choice on how to deal with the situation. I had been beaten by family members, so to me it was a simple equation: bully + punch + pencil = stabbing. The only problem was that, in the moment, I didn't consciously solve that equation. I didn't *choose*. Instead, I just reacted as though the only potential outcome of the situation was me stabbing the bully.

If someone would have asked me, "why did you stab that kid?" my response may very well have been, "I didn't have a choice." Ever find yourself saying that to yourself or to others? If so, then like me, you would have been wrong. It would be more accurate to say, "I didn't realize that I had a choice."

I'm not saying that stabbing that kid wasn't the right decision. I'm just saying that it wasn't a decision at all—it was merely a reaction. What else might I have done? I was quick enough to dodge the kid's punch. I was much faster than he was—it would have been an easy thing to run to safety. Or I could have called for help. But those options never crossed my mind. I only reacted. Swing, dodge, stab.

Contrast that experience with the following story. Fast forward six years. I am nearly thirteen. My mother had passed away and my father's parental rights had been terminated. Before she died, my mother asked the state of Hawaii to transfer me and my siblings to Utah, where she had family. The state granted her request, and we moved from my home state to the mainland across the Pacific. By this time, my four younger brothers and sisters were in permanent placements with three different families. I, on the other hand, had changed homes fifteen times.

There was a different reason for each change—my lashing out at other children in the home; my foster family going on an expensive summer vacation that didn't include a foster kid tag-along; foster parents' struggles dealing with my hyperactivity; my desire to live in closer proximity to one or more of my siblings; and so on.

For my thirteenth birthday, my foster parents gave me a book of a compilation of dozens of Native American myths. I had expressed interest in my heritage, which I knew little about, other than my father's claims that he was part Cherokee. As I read the book, I was surprised to find my father's name listed as the contributor of several of the myths.

I hadn't spoken to my father since his parental rights had been terminated over three years earlier. I was curious, however, to find out how my father's name came to be listed in this book on Native American stories. At that time, my foster parents' marriage was on the rocks, and a troubled teenager wasn't what they needed. They encouraged me to reunite with my biological father, whom I had not even seen in nearly four years.

An uncle, my biological mother's brother, had been friendly with my father, and I found out that he had a telephone number where I could reach my father. We reconnected. It turned out that he was living nearly three hundred miles away in Southern Utah. We arranged a weekend visit. After a few weeks of getting reacquainted with my father, my foster parents and I packed me up, and about one month before I turned fourteen, I went to live with my father and my older brother, who had been living with him for about a year.

We lived in a borrowed double-wide trailer up in the mountains of Southern Utah, fifteen miles outside of Hurricane, Utah where I attended school. Although I felt a sense of belonging returning to my father and brother, it was not an ideal living situation for a young teenager. The good news was that, by then my father had enough control over his anger issues that his physical abuse of my brother

Our borrowed trailer in Apple Valley, Utah

and me appeared to be a thing of the past. The bad news is that we didn't have much by way of food, clothing, heat, or parental attention. None of those deficiencies bothered my father much. My brother and I got by working odd jobs or relying on the generosity of friends' families.

Our double-wide was off of a dusty compacted dirt road, just over a mile from the highway that would take us down the mountain and into town. Pretty desolate, surrounded by dust, desert grasses, sage brush and juniper trees. Lots of rabbits, spiders and bats to keep us company.

For large chunks of time, including many nights, my father wasn't at the trailer. He had remarried, and his wife lived with her adult son in a neighboring town down in the valley. He spent most nights with her, while my brother and I lived in the trailer with a couple of dogs and a crazy cat.

Although Southern Utah is known for being warm all year around, the mountain where we lived? Not so much. During the winter months, the temperature overnight would drop well below freezing. Our trailer's only source of heat was a small, black, cast iron stove at the front of the trailer, and the coal we used in the stove to heat the home would never last a winter night. My brother and I would trade off nights adding coal to the stove when we inevitably woke from the cold to take the edge off the frigid air as we slept.

My brother was sixteen and had a driver's license. My father had a relationship with the owner of a used car dealership, who loaned us a car to get around in. That was helpful for a time, but unfortunately, my brother wrecked that car while driving late one night on the narrow winding roads near Zion National Park. Thankfully, he was okay, but with the borrowed car totaled, the only way to get to school was to hike to the bus stop a mile away. And if I missed the bus? Hitchhiking to school. Not the safest form of transportation for a fourteen-year-old kid.

With my father staying with his wife much of the time, there was *very* limited parental supervision. You can probably imagine what kind of trouble a couple of wayward teenage boys might get into when left to their own devices for extended periods of time. Without going into any specifics, whatever you imagine—there's a good chance you are probably right. (I said the cat was crazy. *Maybe* he was crazy because after a couple rounds of poker, somebody wanted to see if marijuana has the same effect on felines as it does on humans. It doesn't… or so I have been told.)

One afternoon, after I had lived in Southern Utah for about six months, my father and I were driving up the mountain towards the trailer (in another borrowed car, one that my brother was *not* allowed to drive). As we pulled off the highway and onto the dirt road towards our place, he dropped a bomb on me. He said, "Robert, we need to talk. I think that it's time to bring your younger brothers and sisters home to live with us."

I was completely dumbfounded. Surely, he was joking. Not only did we not have a "home" so much as we had borrowed shelter, but we barely had the necessities of life. The only reason I had clothes that fit my lanky frame after a significant growth spurt in the prior few months was because a friend's mother saw my need and gave me some of her older son's clothes.

What was more, food was scarce because money was scarce. My father didn't have a steady job that I knew of. If he did, he spent his money on something other than food. Once while he and I were grocery shopping, I picked up the bare essentials—milk, whole oats, eggs, and bread. When we tried to check out with the cashier, the cost was more than my father had. I returned the oats. That was a long walk back to the cereal aisle. I realized that this wasn't a situation where my father had forgotten his wallet or left his cash at home; we simply didn't have any more money. And he wanted to bring my younger brothers and sisters to this?

His parental rights had been terminated nearly five years before. My younger siblings were all in real homes and they had families who loved them. They belonged somewhere. One brother had been adopted four years before—how in the world did he think he was going to get him back? My two younger sisters were on the verge of being adopted together by a loving couple. They had stable and safe families. They had futures. And he wanted to take them away from those families, those futures—that stability—and come to *this*? I thought he had lost his mind.

I told my father, as kindly as I knew how, that his idea was a bad one. I don't know what he expected, but apparently, it wasn't resistance on my part. He demanded to know why I felt that way, so I told him. I pointed out our lack of basic necessities, and our lack of supervision.

He did not like that. Not at all. He wasn't going to be told by a fourteen-year-old "punk" (one of his preferred terms for disrespectful youth like me) that he was an insufficient provider. He got angry. Very angry. Once we got to the trailer, I got out of the car to retreat into my room. But he followed me and continued the argument just inside the trailer door. And once his temper escalated, mine did as well. After some back and forth, in an attempt to show me how much progress he had made as a parental figure, he yelled, "why do you think I don't beat you and your brother anymore?"

I had virtually no mind-mouth filter at the time, so I shot back, "because we're bigger than you." I was 5'11" and my older brother was 6'1". Now, while it was true that we both were *taller* than him by a couple of inches, there is a difference in physical power between an athletic 14-year-old boy and a fully-grown man. At the time, I didn't appreciate that difference. Using a few demeaning words, my father tried to provoke me into turning our argument physical. "You think you're tough? Go ahead and take your best shot." I don't know that I had ever backed down from a fight before, and I wasn't about to back down then.

As I clenched my fist to take my first swing, an unbidden thought flashed through my mind: "*You are about to hit your father.*" In that split second, it seemed that time stopped, and while the world paused, I realized something I had never fully comprehended before: I had a choice.

I didn't *have* to hit him. Yes, I was angry. Yes, he had hurt me repeatedly in the past, so giving it back to him would feel like some form of justice. Yes, everything in my body and emotions told me that I should beat him down. And he was literally asking me to do it. But for the first time, I was keenly aware that I didn't *have* to do what my emotions told me was natural. I had a choice. I got to decide.

With this new realization came a new power—immediate and immense. I had a host of options available to me. I could slug him across the face (or kick him in the nuts). I could use my relatively quick wit to respond verbally to try to provoke *him*. I could ignore him and walk to my room at the back of the trailer. I could leave the trailer and cool off. I could leave and do something else.

I did not have to do what *he* wanted me to do, and I did not have to do what my first instinct seemed to demand that I do. After a few short moments of deliberation, and without a word of explanation, I turned away from him, and walked back out the trailer door. I made my way about a half mile away to my nearest friend's house with a telephone, and I called the police. Within 30 minutes, I had been picked up, and soon was on my way back into state custody.

I do not know what would have happened if I had thrown that punch. Had I reacted like the six-year-old me who stabbed the bully and punched my father, perhaps well-intentioned adults would have viewed my actions with some level of understanding and tolerance due to my troubled background. However, I am glad that I didn't throw that punch. I am grateful that, in that split second, I realized I had a choice, and I chose a better path.

That choice did not immediately show itself as the right one. The responding officer took me back to my father and allowed him to explain the situation. My father convinced the police officer that I was mentally unstable and needed to be immediately admitted to a mental facility.

The officer nearly turned me back over to my father's custody, until I explained forcefully that my father's parental rights had been terminated by court order several years before and he wasn't legally my parent. The officer consulted with his superiors, and ultimately they decided that I should be evaluated for mental fitness.

An emergency evaluation was set up at the nearest major city, Saint George, Utah, and I spent about an hour speaking with a psychiatrist who was tasked with determining whether I should be admitted to a mental institution for a further psychiatric evaluation. Thankfully, the doctor was convinced that I was a *relatively* normal kid. He asked me to step out of his office while he made a call. I knew that I had "passed" his examination because after a few minutes, I heard him yelling something about some bastard trying to ruin a good kid's life. The police decided to turn me over to social services, and I was placed in an emergency group foster home for a few weeks.

That day was a gift to me. I am beyond grateful that I was lucky enough to realize that I had the power to choose how I would respond to a difficult circumstance. Although I could not necessarily choose what happened to me, I had the power to decide how I would act in the face of my circumstances. That has made all the difference in my life. It will make all the difference in your life as well. You must understand that you have the power to choose your own path, your own actions, your own reactions. With that knowledge comes immense freedom.

Now a warning: inevitably linked to the comprehension that you have the power to choose is the often-uncomfortable truth that you are responsible for the results of your decisions.

Once I understood that I had the ability to decide my own fate, that meant that I couldn't blame my poor choices on my difficult past. I could no longer justify losing my temper because I was beaten as a child. I could no longer be excused for treating others without respect because I had been neglected and abandoned. I couldn't justify objectifying women because that had been modeled for me, or because I had been sexually molested and introduced to pornography in my earliest years.

I had to own the results of my actions. Of course, the trauma of my childhood informed my tendencies, and unhealthy coping and survival mechanisms had been developed that needed to be addressed. But at my core, I knew that I was responsible for my choices—both the good, and the bad.

And just because I became empowered with the knowledge that I had choices does not mean that I always chose well. Very often, I didn't. I made bone-headed decisions. I still *make* bone-headed decisions. I didn't always treat others with the dignity they deserved by virtue of their humanity. I screwed up, and I screw up—a lot. But they are my screw ups. No one else's.

That said, I became more mindful of my decisions, and as I was more conscious of my decisions, I started making better choices. The first thing that improved was my schoolwork. Before the confrontation with my father, my report cards had an A or two with a few Cs and Ds to bring down the average. Not a great start to high school. I realized that if I wanted to choose a better future, I would have to do better in school. Immediately after that fateful argument, my grades went up. During the next school quarter—the fourth quarter of my freshman year—and every quarter in high school thereafter, I chose to get straight As.

While choosing to get better grades was important, as I'll discuss in Chapter 6, the most important and valuable choice that I was now empowered to make was that of my own identity. Until that day, I had identified myself as a victim. A victim of my father's cruelty and neglect. A victim of the state that took me from my mother and siblings. A victim of my foster families who I believed didn't understand me. A victim of fate who took my mother from this world.

Now, I was no longer a victim. I chose to be something else. A student. An athlete. A friend. Eventually a husband and a father. I got to choose. I get to choose, every day. And so do you.

You have been victimized, but you are not a victim if you choose to not be one. You may have had no choice in the situations you faced, but you can choose to view yourself as a victim of your childhood or you can choose to view yourself as you truly are—a human being with immeasurable inherent value capable of experiencing, having, and giving love, respect, and happiness.

I am not asking you to deny or ignore the harsh circumstances of your past. I am not telling you to downplay the difficulties and the trauma that you have faced. Being removed from what you knew to be home, and then moved again, and likely again, is a trauma most don't have to shoulder. Whether you grew up physically, sexually, or emotionally abused, or were neglected by those responsible for your well-being, you have been forced to deal with hard things. Yet, surviving trauma—those horrible things done *to* you— need not dictate how you view yourself, and it certainly does not need to dictate how you act. *You* get to choose.

Now, I am painfully aware that the trauma you faced as a child can lead you to be naturally reactive, making it difficult to fully embrace your power of choice. Do not ignore that potential reality. But just because it is *difficult* to embrace your ability to dictate your own fate, does not mean that it is impossible. After all, you have chosen to read this book. You want to choose success. So I know that you can choose to seek help resolving your childhood trauma.

If you find that you are highly reactive to stressful circumstances like I was, or that you feel that you do not have the power to get past your trauma, seek assistance. Find a mental health provider that specializes in trauma recovery. I am not an expert in trauma recovery treatments, and this book is not the place to try to explain current modes for helping overcome trauma. I only want to encourage you to feel comfortable seeking such help from competent professionals. By virtue of being a foster child in the United States, you have access to such providers, even for a few years after aging out. I have personally used trauma recovery mental health professionals, both as a foster child and as an adult. They can help you fully unlock your ability to choose not to be a victim. You can make that choice.

I carry a reminder of my need to make that that choice every day. When I was about five years old, my father went into one of his fits of rage. I have no idea what set him off (and frankly, it does not matter: it is never okay for a parent to beat his or her child). As his fury flooded through him, he unleashed it on me, and I found myself hurtling end-over-end through our apartment as he kicked me down the hall. Something sharp caught me across the face and split my cheek open.

I don't know what stopped the onslaught—perhaps the sight of his bleeding child. I really don't recall. But I do vividly recall the feeling of fear and helplessness as I twisted through the air, and I can still feel the searing pain burning through my cheek. I remember the feeling of betrayal and shame, wondering why he would hurt me like that and erroneously believing to my core that it must be my fault. Almost forty years later, those feelings and memories are still there.

The scar from that incident can still be seen across my right cheek. Although it is deep and fairly wide, over the years, the color has faded. Somebody looking at me wouldn't likely even notice it if he or she didn't know its story. But I see it every time I look in the mirror. Every time I shave, my razor passes over that scar. It could be a constant reminder of what he did to me; what he took from me. But it's not. Most of the time, it is just there. Each morning as I wash away the shaving cream, and pat on some aftershave, I don't dwell on the pain that it represents. I have never ignored or denied its presence. I choose not to dwell on it. Every day I choose to not let that scar, or my past, define who I am by dictating my decisions for me. I get to decide my actions.

You can do the same. You can choose to let your past repeatedly victimize you, or choose to rise beyond that. You can choose to be whoever you want to be. Your greatest tool in having a successful life is understanding and acknowledging to yourself, to your very core, that you have the power to choose. When you acknowledge that, decide today to choose a life of success.

CHAPTER 3

FIERCELY GUARDING YOUR ABILITY TO CHOOSE

Hopefully, by now you recognize that you have the power to do "it"—to find and have success in life, however you define that. And you understand that you have the power to consciously choose that successful life. That power of choice is the greatest gift you have. This is the core concept on your road to success, but for some it may be the most difficult to follow. It's your responsibility to guard that ability to choose, and it's critical that you do.

What does this mean? It means that all of those things that reduce your freedom of choice *are not for you*. It's essential that you avoid anything that can lead to any sort of physical, emotional, or behavioral addiction.

Addiction is a bit of a scary word. And in today's usage, it is often loaded with all sorts of stigma and connotations. That said, what do I mean by addiction? When I use the word "addiction," I refer to any behavior that is compulsive enough to negatively impact your ability to choose a successful life. However, given the fact that there are countless books written on the subject of addiction, most of which are written by people far more expert in the field than me, I am going to only touch on those addictions that are particularly prevalent and destructive to you as you age out of foster care: substance addiction, and pornography addiction.

Substance Abuse

Substance addiction is characterized by compulsive substance use despite harmful consequences. When you allow yourself to consume substances that can potentially lead to addiction, what you are really doing is risking your ability to choose, the most important thing you need in order to succeed.

According to the American Psychiatric Association, people can develop addictions to a host of substances, including:

- Alcohol
- Marijuana
- PCP, LSD, and other hallucinogens
- Inhalants, such as paint thinners and glue
- Opioid pain killers, including codeine, oxycodone, heroin
- Downers – sedatives and hypnotics such as amorbarbital, and phenobarbital
- Cocaine, methamphetamine and other stimulants
- Tobacco

While there are admittedly several appropriate uses for many of these substances, experimenting with them recreationally, or otherwise misusing them can lead to an addiction that can weaken your ability to choose success.

Pornography Abuse

Today, I don't believe that any discussion with teenagers and young adults about harmful behavior can be complete without discussing behavioral addiction to pornography. Although the effects of compulsive pornography use have not been studied as thoroughly as substance abuse, it is now well-established that regular viewing of online pornography can lead to behavioral addiction. I identify compulsive pornography use specifically because of the significantly higher than average likelihood that youth in foster care have suffered some form of sexual abuse in their past.

For those of us with trauma—and especially sexual trauma—in their past, online pornography can be a relatively inexpensive and readily available substitute to confronting and moving past our pain. Abuse involves a betrayal or failure of human connection. Victims of abuse frequently need help restoring that connection. Human intimacy and sexuality are intended to combine in a supreme expression of human connection. Pornography removes the intimacy and connection otherwise available from healthy sexual relationships thereby potentially robbing its consumers of that intimate connection.

Possibly worst of all, online pornography perpetuates unrealistic or unhealthy views and expectations of sexual relationships that may already have been formed by sexual abuse, including the false belief that either you or your potential partner is nothing more than an object designed to satisfy another's sexual urges.

I encourage you to avoid pornography, and instead seek real human connection. You cannot afford to allow periodic exposure to pornography (which is virtually certain in this digital age) to turn to addictive consumption of counterfeit connection.

———————— ❊ ————————

Regardless of the type of addiction, people with addictive disorders often have distorted thinking and behavior. Frequently, individuals suffering from substance addiction are rendered unable to see positive aspects in people or situations, focusing only on the negative. This can lead to unreasonably exaggerating the negative aspect of oneself, undervaluing oneself and mistaking *feelings* of inadequacy (which we all have from time to time) with *facts*, believing that oneself actually *is* inadequate, which couldn't be further from the truth.

Brain imaging studies of persons with substance abuse addictions show changes in the portions of the brain that relate to judgment, decision making, learning, and behavior control. In other words, substance and behavioral addictions impair your ability to choose. If you surrender your ability to choose, you have given up your greatest tool in your quest to rise above the trauma of your youth.

I understand the draw of addictive substances. They are a form of self-medication that can make you temporarily feel better and dull the pain of loss and stress. I don't doubt that given your background you could use a little something to help you feel good, or a little something to help you avoid your pain. But for you, the risk of addiction is too great because you need your healthiest mind and body to make the choices necessary to be successful.

You must steer clear, at all costs, of any substance or behavior that can cause addiction. While others your age may be able to dabble in these substances and come out relatively unscathed, it's a risk that you need to decide you cannot afford to take. You are already playing the game of life with a short deck—not through any fault of your own, but because of the decisions of adults who should have put you and your needs above their own but were unable or unwilling to do so. While you mature and work through the loss, abuse, and trauma you have suffered, you cannot compromise your ability to make decisions. You cannot compromise your ability to choose to not be a victim.

My four younger siblings were adopted into three different homes, while my older brother, my older sister, and I were not, and aged out of the system. My brother Kurt, who is less than a year younger than I am, was the first of my siblings to be adopted. He was ten years old when his journey in foster care ended through adoption. His adoptive parents gave him a comfortable and relatively stable adolescence. Like me, he had been a victim of physical abuse in our home. Some of it was so vicious that it left his body scarred.

Kurt struggled. As a young adult, he left his adoptive family to return to the island of our birth in Hawaii. He began exploring and abusing different substances: alcohol, meth, cocaine, and a variety of other street and prescription drugs. I was already married at that time, and my wife and I were expecting our first son. We lived about forty-five minutes south of Salt Lake City, Utah.

Two days before I was scheduled to take the LSAT, the Law School Admission Test, I got a call from my brother. He confessed that for the past six months he had been abusing alcohol and drugs, and that under their influence he had participated in exceptionally risky sexual behaviors. He needed help to get away from the party scene.

My wife and I didn't have a lot of spare money, but we agreed that we would help him get away from the influences that were contributing to his dangerous choices. We purchased a one-way ticket from Honolulu to Salt Lake City for him.

The next day I picked him up at the airport, and as I drove him to our apartment, we talked. We talked all day. He told me about how tough it had been for him when our mother died. We talked about the abuse, and how bad it sucked to have been raised in foster care and raised apart from each other. We talked about the pain of watching our older sister suffer from Multiple Personality Disorder due to her childhood abuse, and the pain of dealing with the aftermath of her suicide when we were teenagers. My brother told me about his struggles to fit in with his adoptive family, and his decision to move back to Hawaii.

He told me about the drugs, the drinking, and the sex. It didn't start with the hard stuff. He was an adult and could legally consume alcohol. But drinking turned to drinking in excess. At drunken parties, people started popping pills and passing pipes. He joined in. More dangerous substances quickly followed, and soon he was trapped in a cycle of darkness and despair. Six months into this new lifestyle, he realized that he was miserable. He realized that his choices would lead to more pain. So he asked for help.

I commended him for reaching out. We talked about a plan. (In fact, we talked about each of the principles in this book.) He needed to find a way to serve other people, and he needed to start getting an education. Although he had graduated from high school, I knew that in order to best provide for himself, he needed to get further training. My

wife and I told him that we would help him find an apartment and help him cover the security deposit and the rent
while he found a job. We helped him start his application to
the local community college.

When midnight came, I told him I had to get to bed
because I had a really important test to take the next morning. After a poor night of sleep, morning came, and I went
to take the LSAT. I was a pretty distracted, and I knew that I
didn't do as well as I could have. (Thankfully, when my score
came back, it was enough to get admitted to law school.)

When I returned home after taking the test, I found that
my brother had packed up his things. Confused, I asked him
where he was going, and he told me that he had purchased
a ticket to go back to Hawaii. He was leaving that evening.
I was shocked.

I tried to convince him to stay and follow the plan that
we had discussed. I begged him, saying, "Kurt, nothing you
have done has to dictate the rest of your life. If you turn your
life around right now, years from today you'll look back and
say, *man, that was just a dumb six months of my life.*" His
response broke my heart:

"Rob, if I turn my life around in eighteen months from
now, years from then I'll look back and say, *man, that was
just a dumb two years of my life.*" With that he left. His plan
was to sow his wild oats for two years, and then flip a switch
and live a productive life.

Unfortunately, that's not how substance abuse works. For fifteen years, Kurt was consumed by his addictions. We stayed in contact and saw each other as often as occasions would permit. He never started his advanced education, though he always seemed to have plans to apply to one school or another. He was rarely able to hold a job for more than a few months. He experienced drug-induced comas and had several close brushes with death. He did rehab, then relapsed, hit rock bottom, and did rehab again.

On July 31, 2017, I received a call from my youngest sister. None of Kurt's friends had seen him for over a week; the last day anyone had any contact with Kurt was on July 21. It had been over two weeks since I had spoken with him. He had not posted anything on his Facebook page for weeks.

We decided that we should send the police over to his apartment to check up on him. My sister called the Honolulu Police Department and asked them to go by his apartment. There, they found his lifeless body, slumped in his bathroom. An autopsy confirmed that he had died from meth poisoning 7–10 days earlier.

My sister's call came while I was on a business trip to train my company's employees about our company's new insider trading policy. My company had just gone public on the NASDAQ Stock Market ten days before—the last day anyone had spoken with Kurt. The oldest of my three sons, fifteen years old at the time, accompanied me.

After my first training session, my son and I grabbed a quick lunch at Wendy's. My sister's call reporting what the police had found came as we finished our meal. "Kurt is dead," she cried. "They found his body."

Kurt is dead. My little brother was dead. Head swimming, dazed and temporarily numb, I sent a quick text to a business colleague to say that due to a personal emergency, I would miss a previously scheduled conference call, then I drove to the hotel with my son. There, I broke down in sobs and began the process of mourning the loss of another sibling.

I am glad that my son was with me. I don't think that he had ever seen his father cry before, and as hard as it must have been for him, it was good for him to see the importance of being able to feel pain, and to process grief. Choosing to move past pain and suffering does not mean ignoring it. You recognize pain, you feel it, you process it. If needed, you seek professional assistance in dealing with your grief. There is absolutely no shame in that. And then you consciously decide to move forward. I am grateful that my son got to see that it is okay to feel and express emotional anguish.

Two years before he died, my brother and I were at lunch together. We hadn't seen each other for some time, and it was good to catch up. We spoke about his drug use. He told me, "You know, Rob, I think the main reason I have struggled with drugs so badly is because of the abuse we faced as kids, because of the abandonment I felt, and because I wasn't able get along with my adoptive father." I did not respond; I just looked at him intently to see if he could recognize the flaw in his statement. It took several moments, but he eventually amended his statement with "and my choices, too."

Kurt's substance abuse didn't only deprive him of the ability to choose to get an education or to sustain a job. It deprived him of the ability to choose not to be a victim of our childhood. It robbed him of the ability to choose a successful life. In the end, it robbed him of his life in its entirety.

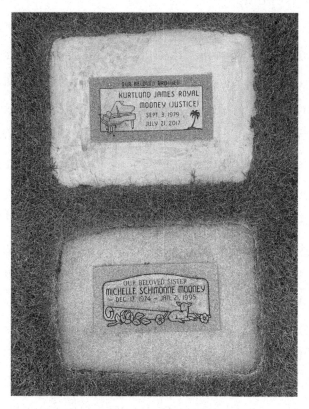

Provo, Utah, the final memorial for my older sister and younger brother, where they share a gravesite.

My friend, you need to guard your ability to choose as though it is your most valuable possession. Because it is. Stay far, far away from any substance that can compromise your ability to choose. That may be hard. Many of you will have seen your own family members use or abuse drugs and alcohol. Some of you will have been intentionally exposed to pornography by parents or guardians. All of you have been subjected to enough pain and suffering that the promise of escaping that pain, even if only temporarily, may seem so very tempting.

If you choose to consume drugs (whether street or prescription), pornography, alcohol, or tobacco, some people would excuse your choice. They might say it would be understandable given your background and experiences. In fact, given that a significant percentage of foster care placements are necessitated by caregiver substance abuse issues, chances are pretty high that addictive behaviors have been modeled for you by a parent or sibling. But as I said before: I expect more from you. I know that you have the power to overcome your past. You are needed to be an example to others on how to overcome hard things.

You may be reading this book thinking, "Rob, it is too late. I'm already using drugs/tobacco/alcohol/pornography." I have good news for you. It is not too late. It's hard, but it's not too late. I know of many others who were able to turn away from years of addiction to lead productive lives.

You have access to addiction therapists and programs. Seek out those programs.

You can regain your full power of choice, but you need to do it now. You may need help and that's ok. There is no need to try to shoulder your burden alone. Look past yourself and reach out. There are people who are there to help you.

Remember that your greatest ability is your power to choose, and you have the power to choose to avoid these substances. You have the power to turn away from these substances. And you have the power to seek help to overcome these substances. If necessary, regain, and thereafter fiercely defend your ability to choose.

CHAPTER 4

YOU ARE NOT ALONE

I've found that if there is one feeling that is nearly universal among teenage foster kids, it is a frequent feeling of profound loneliness.

When you wake up in the morning in a home where you feel like an outsider, you feel alone. When you think on your parents' inability or unwillingness to care for you, you feel alone. When you remember your parents' unwillingness to do what it takes to get you back, you feel abandoned and desperately alone. Sometimes that feeling of loneliness can be absolutely debilitating. I know that loneliness. But I discovered that I wasn't truly on my own. Even when I felt like I had nobody, the reality was this: I was not alone. This discovery came through two distinct events.

A Teenager's Prayer

After that watershed year living with my biological father and brother, I returned back to the Wasatch Front (the Salt

Lake City/Provo area), where I had lived in a few different foster homes for four years before moving to live in Southern Utah. I called one of my best friend's parents, let them know I needed a place to stay, and asked if I could come live with them for a bit. Before I had moved to live with my father, their home had been something of a refuge for a number of their teenage sons' friends, including me. Their table, home and hearts were always open. I wasn't surprised when they welcomed me to come live with them—that's just the kind of people they were. Both parents were beloved schoolteachers in the valley where they lived.

Given the fact that I had been off DCFS's radar for nearly a year (my return to my biological father was not sanctioned by the state), it took a little bit of time for my friend's family to be legally appointed as my foster parents. I was assigned a new case worker, Jayne Carlton, who began to prepare me to transition to adult living. I turned fifteen shortly after moving in with my friend's family.

Living with this new foster family met so many of my physical and emotional needs. I was safe, I was cared for, and I was loved. I had opportunities to participate in sports and other extracurricular activities (all of their kids were exceptionally athletic and active). Both parents seemed like they spent most of their time at ball parks, basketball games or gymnastic meets, always supporting their kids. I could not have asked for better foster parents for that period in my life. They opened their home and helped me escape my prior toxic living situation with my father.

That said, while I was there, I felt like an outsider—like I was living with a friend's family, which of course, I was. I wanted to feel like I had a family of my own—a place where I truly belonged. One day it dawned on me that the first family I could truly call my own would likely be the family I created as an adult.

One day after school, I was hanging out with a group of guys. One of them started to complain about how strict his parents were. The conversation quickly sunk into a gripe session during which most of my friends expressed how much they hated their mom or dad, or how much their brothers and sisters bugged them. I didn't say anything. I listened and felt jealous.

Later that day, when I was alone with one of my buddies, I told him that it really bothered me how the guys complained about their families when having a family to call my own was the one thing I wanted more than anything. He didn't justify our friends' bad attitudes or harsh words. Instead, he said, "Rob, if you really want a family, you can ask God for one."

I had never thought that God could possibly be a source to satisfy my deepest desire to have a home and family to call my own. My different foster families had varying religious beliefs systems, ranging from Catholicism, to other varied

Christian faiths, to Buddhism, to no particular faith at all. My biological mother had been born and raised as a member of the Church of Jesus Christ of Latter-Day Saints, and although my father had converted to her faith for a time, he mostly adhered to his own brand of Native American Spiritualism. While I identified most closely with my mother's faith, I was not living the tenants of that faith and had not fully internalized spirituality in my life. But as I thought about my friend's advice, I realized that I really didn't have anything to lose by asking God for a family.

And so I did. That night, I said a pretty basic prayer that went something like this: "God, my buddy tells me that you can give me a family. So, if you are there, and you are listening, I'd like one."

The very next day, guess what happened? *Nothing.*

I don't really know what I was expecting. I had spent over nine years in the foster care system, so I figured I could give God a little time. That next night, I said pretty much the same thing. "God, I hear you can give me a family. So, if you are there, and you are listening, I'd really like one." I repeated the same prayer for days, and then weeks, and then months.

Shortly after school was out and summer began, I got a call from Jayne Carlton. Since getting my case the previous year, Jayne had been a fierce advocate for me. I knew she was working hard to find me a permanent home, but there weren't a lot of people looking to foster a high school boy with my troubled background. That day, however, she said something that made my heart stop: "Rob, I think I found you a home. They want to meet you."

Jayne came to pick me up to meet the new family. They lived about fifteen minutes from my current placement. The first thing I noticed as we drove into their neighborhood was that it was in a really, *really* nice part of town. Beautiful homes. Meticulous lawns and landscaping. As we pulled up to the family's house, I was amazed. It was, in my mind, a mansion—complete with a swimming pool, and outdoor basketball and tennis courts. My only thought was, "whoa, God is hooking me up. This prayer thing might really work!"

If the house and grounds were amazing, they were nothing compared to the people that lived there. The family. Potentially *my* family. The mother and father were both exceptionally kind. They greeted me with the warmest of smiles, like they had waited their whole lives to meet me. What's more, like me, they were very high energy, outgoing individuals.

They had three daughters; one who had already graduated from high school, one who would be a senior the following school year, and one who would be a sophomore. Although they lived in the same city where I had lived the prior school year, we attended different high schools, and I did not know the girls.

They also had a younger son, who had always wanted an

older brother. I connected with everyone with ease.

They told me that they recognized bringing me into their home permanently was a huge commitment and they wanted to take their time getting to know me. Questions needed to be resolved in their minds and their hearts. How would I interact with their son? Would I be a good role model for him? How would I interact with their daughters? Would they be safe with me in the home?

They were candid about the role that faith played in their lives, and they made it clear that they wanted time to pray and ponder about the potential placement to determine whether they felt it was God's will for me to join their family. That didn't bother me at all—it was clear to me that they were the answer to my prayer, so if it took some time for them to get their answer, that was fine by me.

Over the next couple of weeks, I spent a lot of time with my potential family. I swam in the pool, played basketball with the father and son, met other teenagers in the neighborhood, played various board games with the family, and even went boating with them. If my time as a foster kid had been a Hallmark movie, this would have been the perfectly scripted conclusion with a fairy tale ending.

Or so I thought.

After a few weeks of these "getting to you know you" activities, they invited Jayne and me to a family meeting. I realized that something was seriously wrong when I saw the mother and son. They each had tears in their eyes. A feeling of dread came over me: that anxiety that starts to numb feeling and hollow out your stomach when you know something bad is going to happen.

The dad reminded me that part of the reason we had spent so much time together was so they could get to know me. They had come to the conclusion that I would get on perfectly well with their son, and that they felt comfortable with how I interacted with their daughters.

But then he reminded me that they also wanted to make sure that taking me in was God's will. This was the sticking point. They told me that I *wouldn't* be coming to live with them—they did not feel that it was God's plan to have me become part of their family.

I was devastated, hurt and embarrassed. I was angry. As I processed his words, I felt tears burning to gush out, and I dropped my head and covered my eyes just in case I wasn't able to keep them in.

It felt like something beyond amazing had been held out to me, and just as I reached to take it for my own, it was pulled back, with a sardonic "Just kidding, loser." I felt rejected again, and even surrounded by people, I felt that deep, dark, loneliness with which I was so familiar. The meeting wasn't long—less than a half-hour—but the minutes dragged out painfully before I could retreat somewhere to be alone with my grief.

Before Jayne and I left to return me to my friend's home, the dad told me, "Rob, the only reason why you aren't supposed to come live with us is because either God has more for you to learn from your experience, or because he has something better in store for you."

I knew that he meant well, but his words brought no comfort. I couldn't imagine a better place for me. As for learning more? I wasn't interested in any additional life lessons that came by virtue of being a cast-off kid with no place to call my own.

That night, I lost faith. Instead of prayers going up to the heavens, the tears I only partly kept from flowing earlier fell freely to my pillow. My only conclusion was that if God did exist, and if He had heard my prayers, then He had a twisted sense of humor. I wasn't interested in what He was planning.

I was so angry and so lonely. But I had already discovered my power of choice. I acknowledged my anger and hurt, then I exercised my power to move beyond the experience. My resolve to make a family of my own as an adult was fortified. That didn't change the loneliness I felt. I knew it would be years before my dream of having a family of my own could be realized, and that felt like a very, very long time.

The family's decision to not take me in was tough on Jayne as well. She genuinely cared about me. She knew that I was probably going to age out of the system, so she re-doubled her efforts to help me prepare to live independently. This included having me attend summer school so that I could graduate from high school early and get a jump start on my post-secondary education before aging out.

A few weeks later, on the Fourth of July, Jayne called me to ask a personal favor. Her next-door neighbors, the Cooks, had an adopted daughter named Kim who was a couple of years younger than I was. Kim's adoptive parents had three biological children, all adults; an older girl and two older boys.

The closest sibling to Kim's age was a brother who was ten years older. He was about to start medical school. Her second brother was already in medical school in Texas, and the oldest, her sister, had already graduated from medical school. All three were married; the youngest of the sons and his wife lived in an apartment attached to the Cooks' home. Kim was the only kid living in the main house.

Jayne told me that Kim was going through some difficult personal issues related to being adopted. Jayne thought that, given my background, I might be able to help Kim, or at least be a friend that she could talk to who might understand some of the struggles that she was having.

That afternoon, Jayne picked me up, and took me to the Cooks' house to meet Kim. Kim had dark hair, dark eyes and olive skin, like me. She clearly had significant Hispanic and/or Native American heritage, like me. I met her parents, who were Caucasian, and her older brother who was visiting from Texas with his wife and two young daughters.

Kim and I spent some time getting to know each other. I learned a bit about her background, and she learned a bit about mine. Even though she had been adopted as a young child, Kim felt like she had trouble fitting in. My years as a foster kid had taught me a little something about that. Unlike all three of her siblings, Kim wasn't inclined towards a career in medicine. That made her feel different. And as the only adopted child in the family, she felt like the odd man out. She didn't look like her parents or her siblings. I could definitely relate there.

We spent hours talking. I don't know that anything I said or did helped her, but after our short time together, I felt that I had made a friend.

A few days later, Jayne called me on the phone. She had some news, along with a confession. She admitted that the purpose of my meeting with Kim had less to do with helping out her friends' daughter, and more with giving the Cooks a chance to meet me and consider whether they wanted to take me in. After meeting me, and seeing me interact with their daughter, the Cooks decided to invite me to come live with them.

When Kim's parents agreed to take me in, they did not intend to adopt me. Rather, their expectation was to provide a stable place for me to transition from foster care to adult living. They knew I was going to be a senior in high school, and that I was likely to be going to college when I graduated.

Even though the Cooks were intended to be a transitional placement and a safe place for me to age out, they eventually became something more. And it turned out that their home actually was the best possible place for me to be. My almost-foster father was right—God did have something better in store for me.

There isn't room here to give an appropriate tribute to the family that I have been part of for over twenty-five years. I could write an entire book about how amazing the Cooks were—and are. I could tell you about everything they taught me, and how they opened their hearts to me. Although they never adopted me, and I moved out for college after living with them for less than a year, the Cooks are the people who my children call Grandma and Grandpa.

As it turns out, the Cooks were exactly what I needed, more so even than the previous family that seemed like the perfectly tailored match. You see, Kim's parents were *not* like me. They weren't high energy, super outgoing people. Growing up as a foster kid, moving from home to home, I usually felt like I was flying by the seat of my pants, evolving and improvising on the spot to keep up with my ever-changing life circumstances. That wasn't how the Cooks operated. Instead, they were reserved, steady, quiet, patient, and hard-working. They had life skills that were wholly missing in my personal development. They helped me model and develop those life skills, making me a more complete person.

Even more important, they had something that helped me feel like I was truly part of a family for the first time. In nearly every prior foster placement, regardless of the quality of my foster parents (and I had some that were exceptional), I almost always felt like I was an intruder on someone else's life. I was an imposter: a fake brother, a fake son. I was a burden. Not with the Cooks. They had Kim.

I moved in with Kim's parents on July 16, less than two weeks after I met the family. Kim and I spent hours upon hours hanging out, talking about life, playing pool, and just getting to know each other. Because Kim and I had similar skin tones, facial features, and eye and hair color, people frequently assumed that we were biological siblings. To Kim, I wasn't some kid her parents had decided to shelter. I was her brother. And notwithstanding the fact that Kim struggled with feeling like she belonged, it was clear to me that, even though she was adopted, she was a treasured member of the family. That helped me feel like I could be part of the family as well.

As I reflected on how I got to the Cooks, starting with a prayer, leading to a potential placement that *seemed* perfect, but was taken away, before being placed with Kim and her family, I realized that God didn't just hear and answer my prayer. He answered my prayer *perfectly*. It turned out that I was *not* alone after all. There was a Divine power that knew me, was watching over me, and was my companion even when I felt I was on my own.

Now, some reading this book may say, "hold on Rob, you can't talk about God and foster care!" My simple response is that it would be irresponsible for me *not* to talk about a foster kid's connection to the Divine. Why? Because it turns out that most kids who age out of foster care successfully recognize some form of a Higher Power as a key factor in their ability to cope with the trauma of their childhood.

Not long ago, while speaking at a summit of foster youth transitioning to adult living, I met Dr. Terri Nicole Sawyer, who was also a speaker at the summit. After hearing my presentation, during which I shared with the group the principles and stories contained in this book, Dr. Sawyer shared with me some findings she discovered during her research for her doctoral program.

For her PhD dissertation, Dr. Sawyer studied the difficulties facing former foster youth as they transitioned into adulthood. She focused on documenting these struggles from the former foster youths' perspectives. Dr. Sawyer noted that much of the prior research performed in this area failed to capture or recognize the individual nature or story of each youth aging out. She created a study that would allow for more in-depth discussion with the study subjects (former foster youth aged 18-26). She drafted twenty-three questions or prompts that would encourage the young adults to share the experiences as they transitioned from foster care to independent living.

There was little surprise in the general categories of the challenges the aged-out youth faced—educational, vocational, housing opportunities, etc. However, what was surprising was how often these former foster youth referenced some form of spirituality as part of their transition to adulthood. They frequently attributed spirituality as a source of coping skills or strength that lessened the difficulties they faced as they transitioned out of foster care. This was a surprise because none of the survey questions or prompts mentioned or suggested spirituality in any form. Dr. Sawyer's dissertation concluded, "Foster youth have the privilege and right to believe as they wish about their own spirituality. Encouraging spirituality is key to helping them have this powerful support in their lives."

Dr. Sawyer's findings were in line with what I had found out when my friend encouraged me to find God by seeking him through prayer.

I am not going to tell you what your spirituality needs to look like. I'm not here to endorse any particular religion or practice. I just need you to know that there is a Divine presence at work in your life. There is some Power that can allow you to feel comfort when you are hopelessly lonely, to help you forgive when you've been wronged, and to heal when you've been hurt. I came to know that, and so can you. And when dark times come—like they have in the past, and most assuredly will in the future, that Divine can fill your life with light. You are not alone.

A Human Connection

The second experience that helped me realize that I wasn't alone came after I had aged out of foster care and was attending college and living on my own.

When I met the Cooks, Kim had two nieces, Ciarah and Cassidy, who were born barely a year apart. Ciarah turned two less than a month before I moved in and Cassidy had just turned one. The girls lived in San Antonio, Texas where their dad was attending medical school.

I became instant friends with the two little girls. Whenever they would visit their Grandma and Grandpa Cook, I would be there to play with them. I was instantly the cool uncle who would throw them around, read to them, play games with them, or run around the house with each of them tucked under one arm. If a visitor came to the house that they didn't know, they would run to me for protection from the stranger. Ciarah and Cassidy were too young to remember life without me, so as far as they were concerned, I had always been part of the family. I wasn't a burden to the girls; I was just their uncle.

Ciarah and Cassidy

Just a few months after moving in with the Cooks, I started applying for college. In deciding where to go to school, I considered a number of universities throughout the country. I thought a lot about going back home to Hawaii for college. Also, given my Native American heritage, a few East Coast schools with loose ties to some Native tribes caught my eye.

However, I didn't want my time with the Cooks to be nothing more than my last foster home on the way to adulthood. I hoped to continue developing my relationship with them, even though I was leaving for college. So, instead of moving across the country to a college on the East Coast or in the middle of the Pacific, I chose to attend Brigham Young University, located less than fifteen minutes away.

My foster dad worked about three minutes from campus, so it would be easy to see him from time to time. As an added bonus for me, when my nieces would come to town for a visit, I could be there.

Like many college kids, I went home for Thanksgiving and Christmas. But unlike most of my classmates, I was going to a family who had only known me for a year. I was something like a stray dog that keeps coming back after you've fed it a few times. I kept developing my relationship with the Cooks, and I got to keep being Ciarah and Cassidy's uncle.

During my freshman year in college, I had some difficulty sleeping. I would stay up late and wake up pretty early. The benefit of my apparent need for less sleep was that I had enough time to attend to a very full class-load, have a Monday through Friday part-time job, and still have a fairly robust social life. My late nights and early mornings annoyed my dorm roommate, so after my first year, I moved into a private room.

During my second year of college, I officially aged out of foster care and was legally on my own. Unfortunately, by that time, I had a seriously hard time falling and staying sleep. I would only be able to sleep an hour or two a night for stretches of three to four weeks at a time.

It wasn't that I didn't want to sleep, or that I wasn't tired. I was completely exhausted nearly all of the time.

I would crawl into bed every night, starved for sleep, but my brain just wouldn't stop, and I couldn't drift off. Unfortunately, it wasn't like I was some mad scientist genius coming up with brilliant concepts or being amazingly productive in the wee hours of the morning. Nope. What kept my mind in a state of perpetual hyperactivity was entirely unproductive. It would just be repetitive loops of what I had been thinking about before trying to go to sleep. Like a 3-minute video clip repeating itself over, and over, and over. If I had been studying financial economics shortly before trying to sleep, the last things I had read about would loop repeatedly in my mind. You would expect that thinking about economics would be enough to put *anyone* to sleep. Not me—the eternal loop kept me wide awake, tossing back and forth in bed as the scene of the day repeated.

Trying to think of something else was useless. If I watched a movie or read a book to coax my mind to replace the repetitive track, when I would try to sleep, some portion of the movie or book would just replay over and over in my mind—some mental glitch keeping my mind on "repeat," preventing me from falling asleep. Counting sheep and mind-wiping exercises were wholly ineffective.

When I finally did sleep, I would wake up again only an hour or two later with the same repeated thoughts cycling through my mind, and further sleep was impossible. The exhausted sleeplessness would last for weeks on end. My body begged for sleep. My mind craved mental quiet.

At first, I thought that it was the absolute worst to wake up with only an hour of sleep. But then the nights started becoming completely sleepless, and I missed being able to get an hour or two of sleep. One day with no sleep bled into two, and then sometimes into three. The longest stretch I had with no sleep started early one Monday morning and ended late the following Thursday evening—over three and a half days with zero sleep.

Human bodies and minds simply are not designed to function with no sleep. Unsurprisingly, my body couldn't keep that up. Eventually, I would just crash. And I mean seriously crash—sleep for twenty hours or more each day for four or five days in a row. It was like a sleep debt that needed to be paid—all at once.

When I hit the crash portion of the cycle, I didn't spend much time out of bed, waking just long enough to eat and do what was necessary to avoid revealing my problem to my friends. Then back to bed and a return to blessed mental blackness. When I was awake during my crashes, it felt like I was looking at the world through darkened, misty glasses. My normally excellent eyesight was replaced with blurry, unfocused visual perception. Just trying to keep my eyes opened gave me intense headaches, especially when I was trying to mask my fatigue from friends.

After spending nearly a week in partial hibernation, I would have a couple of days of "normal" sleep—six or seven hours a night—and then the cycle would start again with one to two hours of sleep a night.

During the first two weeks or so of what I called the "awake" part of my cycle, I was actually pretty productive. I lifted weights, played a lot of basketball, and had a daily running and breakfast date with a close friend. I worked, went to my college classes, and generally enjoyed life.

However, during the last week or two of the cycle, I was so tired that I couldn't focus on anything. I would go to class and work, but I had no ability to absorb anything the teachers said. When trying to read my textbooks, by the time I finished a paragraph, I couldn't remember what I was reading. In fact, I couldn't even be sure if I had actually read the prior paragraph.

Since I was living in a single dorm room, I could keep my condition to myself. Towards the end of each cycle, when I was little more than a zombie, I avoided most social interactions. Although people closest to me could see that something was wrong, nobody really knew what was happening for over a full semester. In college, you generally don't have someone watching over you to make sure you are getting to class. If you don't show up, an attendance cop doesn't come knocking—you just get bad grades.

I told my friends that I just wasn't feeling too well, and

that was enough for most of them. I felt that I had nobody that I could turn to for help. I hid my condition in the shadows, afraid that people would think I was some sort of freak. Like when I was a kid growing up, being passed from foster home to foster home, I felt completely alone. During my moments of greatest extremity, where my mind and body screamed for sleep, I would cry to God for relief. But like those early months of praying for a family, the heavens felt distant and closed.

A few times during the semester, I considered calling my parents to let them know what was going on. But I felt deep shame. All three of the Cooks' older kids had been stellar students and all three were doctors (or on their way to becoming doctors). I wanted to be academically successful like them, and I didn't have the courage to let my parents know that I was struggling.

I had three different jobs that semester because I quit the first two as I was crashing, knowing I would likely get fired for absenteeism. During the first part of each awake cycle, I tried to catch up on the schoolwork that I had missed during the prior crash. However, by the time I was three cycles into the semester, I was failing most of my classes with virtually no hope of catching up. As the end of the semester came, so too did the unproductive end of an awake cycle, followed by a crash to finish the school term. I failed the entire semester. *Zero credit.*

I felt like a complete failure. Worthless. I didn't understand how I could have let this happen to myself. After all, in the several years since I discovered my power to choose my own fate, I had been a perfect, straight-A student. And now I had completely flunked a full college semester.

Right after the university's finals period ended, I received a call from my foster mom. She said, "Rob, Ciarah and Cassidy just got here for Christmas, and the first thing Ciarah said was 'Grandma, where's our friend Rob?' Can I bring them to you for a quick visit?" I eagerly agreed. After I hung up the phone, I buried my head in my pillow in tears. Why? For the first time in four months, I realized that I had a human connection that mattered. These tears were tears of gratitude that these two little girls knew who I was and missed me when I was gone. I wasn't truly alone.

I cleaned myself up and saw my foster mom and nieces for a just a few minutes; just long enough for them to hop out of the car, give me a big hug and discuss a plan of what we would do in the next few days over the Christmas holiday.

Even though I hadn't told my parents how badly I had struggled during that semester, my mom could sense that something was wrong. Somehow, she knew that a visit from my nieces was exactly what I needed. And it made all the difference in the world knowing that those two little girls were in my corner. They wouldn't care that I had failed a semester of college, they just wanted their uncle to play with them. For some reason, having that support gave me the courage to seek help.

Shortly after Christmas, I confessed to my parents that I had failed the semester and explained what had been going on. My confession took them by surprise. They told me that they knew something was off but didn't realize how bad it had been. I think that they were a little hurt that I didn't turn to them for help earlier. To avoid that in the future, they made it clear that I shouldn't feel like I had to shoulder my burdens alone, and that I could turn to them for support. And I did. As I struggled with my symptoms for the next few years, I kept them in the loop, and they were a source of comfort and support.

My parents encouraged me to get professional help. Since aging out, I had been on the university's health plan, so I met with a psychologist, and then a psychiatrist on campus. I was diagnosed with Rapid Cycling Bipolar Disorder, a form of manic depression in which you cycle through periods of mania and depression extremely quickly. Although my symptoms did not fully fit the diagnosis, because my biological parents each had one or more diagnosed mental illnesses, the mental health professionals believed it was the best diagnosis for my symptoms. The psychiatrist prescribed medication to help manage the cycles.

Initially, I was a pretty ashamed to be told that there was something wrong with my brain that caused my crazy sleep cycles. But my doctor put it in pretty simple terms for me. Should I feel ashamed if I had broken my arm and needed a cast? Would there be any shame if I had diabetes and needed insulin? Of course not. So why should I be ashamed to take medication that would treat an illness in my brain?

I started taking the medication. After several years, I eventually was able to manage my sleep cycles with limited prescription assistance. To this day, I still struggle with managing the cycles, but I have learned how to keep them in check. And they haven't kept me from living a fulfilling and productive life, or from having a successful career. But I always remember the isolation I felt while sorting my sleep issues out.

Even if you haven't been diagnosed with an emotional or mental illness, the trauma of your youth has likely led you to feel profound loneliness and alienation. But please believe me, you are not alone. If I had realized that during my failed semester of college, I might not have failed it. I am so grateful that my mom, and those two little girls who never knew life without me, reminded me that there were people who cared about me.

There are people who care about you. Reach out for help when you need it. I have found that most people are inherently good, and are willing to help others in need, if they know that there is a need. There will be help, even though those who come to your aid will be imperfect people.

Even if you can't find people around you to help lighten your load, know that you are not alone. No matter what your spiritual views are, I urge you to recognize the Divine in your life –whether for you that is God, Nature, the Cosmos, Fate, or whatever. That recognition will give you connection. Connection to the Divine, connection with your humanity, and connection with others.

Recognize the Divine. Reach out for help. As you choose to be successful, choose to see that you are not alone.

— CHAPTER 5 —

KARMA IS REAL:
THE LAW OF RECIPROCITY

In Chapter 3, I introduced you to the easiest principle of the road to success to understand, but perhaps the hardest to practice: guarding your ability to choose. In this chapter, I'll discuss the easiest principle to put into practice, but one which may be the hardest for you to internalize.

The principle is simple, and it is iron-clad: If you want to be successful, you need to learn how to freely give to others. There is some force in the Universe that ensures that good is done to those that do good. I call this the law of reciprocity; others call it karma. Some refer to it as the law of the harvest—you reap what you sow. Whatever you call it, the basic idea is this: when you send goodness out into the world, goodness is returned to you. When you send hatred, evil, or bad deeds out into the world, hatred, evil, or bad deeds are returned to you.

That doesn't mean that people who do good only receive good things, or that people who do bad things only experience bad things; you already know that isn't true. Although this law is absolute, it is also subtle in its manifestations in our lives.

When you have been abused, abandoned, or neglected, sending out goodness to the world may be contrary to your instincts. You may have suffered significant periods where you have lacked basic needs. You didn't have enough food, made do with inadequate clothing, lived in unsafe or unsanitary housing. You were deprived of love or affection. When you have lacked the necessities of life, it is understandable to have a compelling urge to stockpile those necessities for yourself once you have access to them. It can be difficult to share what you have. Guarding your resources—physical and emotional—is a natural survival mechanism.

For a short while before I went into foster care, my parents were "in between housing arrangements." Put another way, we were homeless. To be honest, there are worse places in the world than Hawaii to not have a roof over your head. When I was young, there were homeless camps up and down the less commercialized shores of Oahu, and we spent time in one of those camps.

There wasn't a lot of food. However, every day when the tide would go out, the ocean left behind colonies of small black sea snails clinging to the sharp, black lava cliffsides.

You could pop the snails off the rockface with the flat of a knife, and scrape out the salty, slimy insides for something to eat. Some of the camp residents relished the flavor, but I could never get there. I would swallow the slippery flesh without chewing, imagining it leaving a slug's trail of slime down my throat to an empty, waiting stomach. It was pretty gross, but it was food.

When we were back in an apartment, our family was regularly the recipient of the generosity of neighbors, who brought us groceries or made dinners. But sometimes there were empty cupboards and empty stomachs.

For me, the result of those seasons of hunger was a tendency to load up whenever there was food available, and to save some for later if it was possible. That habit followed me for years after my last experience of true extended hunger; I hoarded food in many of my foster homes, hiding food under my bed, on high closet shelves, or inside clothes drawers.

Even after I was eating relatively well, I would sneak food. After I had been in foster care for over four years, I lived with a family with many other children and I shared a basement room with several boys. Next to our bedroom was an unfinished storage room which contained a large freezer. One day, I discovered that the family kept various frozen snacks in that freezer. Even though I always had plenty to eat, in the middle of the night, when the others in my bedroom were asleep, I would sneak to the storage room, and eat some of the snacks they kept in the freezer—while they were still frozen! I don't know if my foster parents ever noticed that the snacks in their freezer were slowly being consumed. If they did, they never called me out on it.

That desire to consume or save excess food follows me, even today. When I practiced law, I had to travel a lot. I racked up a lot of frequent flier miles, and the airline I used the most would usually upgrade me to first class seats when I flew. With my first-class tickets came free meals, snacks and drinks. Every time food would come by, I would have the urge to take some, even if I didn't want it or need it; it was just hard for me to pass up free food. I've learned to master that urge for the most part, but it's still there.

I imagine some of you are the same way. When you have experienced true scarcity, the idea of sharing what you have can be scary. Yes, it's natural to want to consume and keep as much as you can for yourself, but it's important to share what you have with others.

And this applies to far more than food or physical possessions. When you have had really bad things happen to you, it may feel natural for you to be harsh, cruel, or mean to others. But it's important to share kindness with others, even if it feels contrary to your natural desires.

Here's why.

Sir Isaac Newton's Third Law of Motion states for every action there is an equal and opposite reaction. The law of reciprocity could be thought of as a form of mystical physics: for every action you send out, an action is returned to you. But unlike Newton's Third Law, instead of returning an equal and opposite reaction, the law of reciprocity returns an *amplified* version of the goodness you sent out.

Let's say you are going to plant three short rows of corn—ten plants in each row. It doesn't take much of your energy to make a few little furrows and drop in thirty little kernels. With such a small plot, it would take virtually no energy on your part to pull out weeds, and make sure the plants are watered regularly. In about three months you will have thirty stalks, each with one or two ears of sweet corn. During the entire process of planting, caring for, and harvesting that corn, you probably would have expended less than a thousand calories. But in return, you harvested 3,000—6,000 calories of energy, over quadrupling the amount of energy you expended through your efforts.

The law of reciprocity is similar, but in my experience, it is far more generous. It pays out an immediate personal fulfillment and pleasure of doing the right thing, but thereafter, it returns an unpredictable but amplified benefit.

When I moved in with the Cooks, my dad recruited me to help him serve a few families in our neighborhood that he had known for years. One of these was a couple in their early eighties. My dad checked on them periodically and visited with them in their home at least once a month. One dark winter morning, he woke me up well before five o'clock, and told me, "We had a really heavy snowstorm last night." My confused response was, "So what?" "Our friends could probably use someone to shovel their walks and driveway," he told me. "Let's go."

Getting up hours before sunrise on a frigid, snowy morning was not my idea of a good time. That didn't matter; when I moved in with the Cooks, I agreed that I would do my best to do the things they asked of me. I got dressed and joined my dad.

As I shoveled our neighbor's driveway and sidewalk in the muffled quiet of that winter scene with a deep layer of thick soft snow all around me, I was surprised to find that my heart was lightened. As I saw the progress of the walk being cleared, I was filled with the satisfaction of accomplishing something so early in the day. I felt contentment and peace in my heart, knowing that I had done something good for somebody else.

The universe immediately paid me for my good deed, and I've received similar "payments" over and over. In the workplace, I was known as someone who was willing to give ready compliments for a job well done. Every time I did, I felt a sense of peace, knowing that I had spread some good out to the world.

At home, our family delivers home-baked goods to our neighbors (I'm usually a brownie guy, but lately we've been on a jumbo chocolate chip spree). Why? It gives me a chance to bake something with my kids, so that's a bonus. And of course, we get to eat some of what we make—which is definitely nice. But when we take a plate of brownies or cookies to a neighbor to let them know that we are thinking about them, we feel gratified knowing that we brought a little bit of happiness to someone else.

Do you ever feel depressed, lonely, or just a little hopeless? Of course you do. Do you want to feel better? Go out and find somebody to serve.

As satisfying as the way I feel when I do something for someone else, what I find more interesting are the unpredictable and often compounded returns I receive from doing good.

Here's an example. After my second year of college, I felt inspired to take some time off to do some service. Some people do a stint with the Peace Corps, Habitat for Humanity, or Americorps. Others volunteer at hospitals or donate their time to tutor kids. I decided to do a church-service mission. I applied for service and was sent to Boston, Massachusetts for twenty-four months.

In Boston, the mission president who supervised the missionaries sent to Massachusetts assigned me to work in a particular area of the state and assigned me a companion to live and work with. Periodically, the mission president would assign me a new companion, or assign me to a different area of the mission boundaries (my mission covered most of Massachusetts, and small parts of neighboring states).

While I was I missionary, my companions and I volunteered in food pantries, helped prep little league baseball fields, played with kids at the YMCA, and worked in retirement homes entertaining the residents. When we weren't doing secular service, my companions and I would work in our assigned areas—which frequently included rough inner-city neighborhoods—to find people with whom we could share the Gospel. We would work from 9:30 in the morning until 10:00 at night, taking only a half-day off each week to do some grocery shopping, wash our clothes, write home, and relax a little bit.

After living in Massachusetts for about ten months, I was assigned to serve in the Dorchester and Roxbury neighborhoods. At that time, those neighborhoods were pretty dangerous with violent and property crime rates far above the national averages. In Dorchester, my companion and I met a man, probably in his early thirties, who really did not like missionaries. He followed us around the inner-city streets, screaming exceptionally obscene and creative profanities at us. He never physically attacked us, but he occasionally kicked trash at us or lobbed beer bottles near where we walked. Not a friendly guy.

One day, when my companion and I got off the train near our apartment after a long day of work, we saw a nasty fight taking place outside of a bar across the street. A big guy was literally beating the life out of a little guy. As I ran across the street to try to break it up, I could hear the little guy yelling, "I don't know your wife! I don't know your wife!" I assumed that the little guy had made some drunken comment about the big guy's wife, and now he was paying for it by having his face smashed against a brick wall. Blood was everywhere—on the wall, on the big guy's hands, and especially, on the little guy's face.

When I got between them to break it up, the big guy's grip was so tight that he tore off the little guy's shirt as they separated. My companion had followed me across the street. He happened to have a spare t-shirt in his backpack, which he promptly gave the little guy. Instead of putting it on, the little guy used it to wipe the blood off of his face.

We were shocked to see that the little guy was the man who would follow us around screaming profanities at us. We had just saved a guy's life who did everything he could to make us miserable.

My entire time in Massachusetts was spent trying to help people that I did not know—trying to comfort those that stood in need of comfort and bring hope to the hopeless—serving however I could.

What was the law of reciprocity's return for those two years of service? I didn't get paid; not in money anyway. During my missionary years, there were countless examples of immediate Divine reciprocation—that feeling of peace or contentment that comes from doing good. But the most unexpected, and most profitable return came after I returned home.

When I went back to college, I got a job at the training center where new missionaries went to learn about being a missionary before going out to their assigned fields of service. Only people who had already served a church mission could get a job as a missionary trainer.

When I had been working there for only a few weeks, a ridiculously attractive, petite blonde woman approached me and asked, "Hey, didn't you go to Mountain View?" My response was, "Yeah, I did." She followed up: "And didn't you play basketball?" Sound familiar? You may recognize that those were the words I shared at the beginning of this book—the words that re-introduced me to the woman who would become my wife of nearly two decades and the mother of my children.

My dream of having a family of my own was realized; a family that I unquestionably belonged to that I could love, and who could love me. It was made possible in large part because I chose to serve a two-year service mission and taught at the training center when I returned home.

My family

That totally unexpected payout far exceeded any of the good deeds that I did during those two years. Nearly every good thing that has happened in my adult life has sprung from that relationship made possible by my service. But that's how the law of reciprocity works: you send out goodness, goodness is returned to you, usually in entirely unexpected ways. And it is usually far more than what you send out.

You haven't had the advantage of a stable home. You have been hurt, damaged, even broken by those who should have held, guided and protected you. In the game of life, you are playing from behind. Let the law of reciprocity stack the deck in your favor. Start now.

Believe it or not, there are others around you with needs that exceed your own. Choose to serve. Find ways to reach out. Find ways to help. If you look, you will find places around your neighborhood where you can volunteer your time, energy, and skills. And as you do so, the law of reciprocity will begin to work in your favor. You will be paid immediately with peace and positive energy that comes from helping others. In time, you will reap the unexpected rewards that the Universe returns to those who do good. The law of reciprocity is real, and its benefits can be yours if you choose to send goodness out to those around you.

CHAPTER 6

EDUCATION IS KEY

The final key in choosing success is to take your education seriously. Poverty, or the inability to financially provide for the basic necessities of life, is a driving factor in nearly half of all U.S. foster placements. So, chances are pretty good that you have witnessed seeing a parent struggle to pay rent or buy groceries. You likely know what it is like to be hungry. You may know the fear and hopelessness that comes from not knowing where you will lay your head at night.

The single most important factor in avoiding poverty is education. Although you have faced early hardship, you are blessed to live in a society where you have access to educational opportunity. Obtaining a quality education is the key to enable you to provide for yourself and those you love.

Your ability to make money honestly will be linked to what you know and what you can do. Get an education and acquire the skills that society is willing to pay for. In the United States, adults without a high school diploma are by far the most likely to be unemployed. As a rule, average salaries increase as the level of education increases. According to U.S. Census data from 2015, those who did not graduate from high school who are fortunate to be employed make, on average, less than $26,000 a year. With the average rent across the United States for a one-bedroom apartment being about $950 per month, or $11,400 per year, that salary leaves very little for one person after you meet basic shelter and food needs.

Adults *with* a high school diploma have a significantly lower unemployment rate than those without one. They make, on average, just over $35,000 per year. Workers with a two-year associates degree make about $41,500, while workers with a four-year college degree average $59,000 per year. Adults with a master's degree have an average salary of approximately $69,000, and workers with professional degrees (examples would include various medical degrees, law degrees and so forth) make on average $89,000 per year. As a rule, it pays to get more education.

That said, it is certainly not true that the only worthwhile education is a college education. Virtually *any* post-high school training can be valuable. Trade schools—sometimes called vocational, technical, or career schools—offer job-focused training in fields and careers as diverse as IT, medical and dental technicians, and plumbing and electrical work. According to U.S News and World Reports, in 2017, the average annual salary for electricians was approximately $54,000, and the average annual salary for a licensed massage therapist was approximately $40,000. There are a host of vocational training programs that can lead to increased employment opportunities. Find education opportunities relating to your interests and then set your sights on getting as much education as early as possible.

The best way to get a great education is to start now. Whether you are in junior high or high school, you can choose to become a good student. If you've dropped out, you can go for your GED. The sooner you make that choice, the more choices you will have later on.

As I have suggested before, I was not always a stellar student. In fact, before the very end of my freshman year of high school, my grades and overall school performance did not indicate that I was likely to go to college. In fact, one of my teachers thought so poorly of me, that I became a fixture in her classroom folklore of terrible students from years gone by.

When I was a sophomore in high school, I moved back to an area where I had attended seventh and eighth grades. On the first day of school, a friend's younger brother tracked me down and asked, "Hey Robbie! Did you have Mrs. Smith [not her real name] for seventh grade English?"

When I said yes, he informed me, "Today she was explaining the work we would have to do this year. She told us to not be like Robert Mooney, who was the worst student she had ever had in thirty years of teaching."

I was shocked, and terribly embarrassed. Although I knew that I hadn't been a great student, and I knew that this teacher in particular really didn't like me, it was tough to hear the label: Worst. Student. Ever.

You might wonder what I could have possibly done to be singled out by a seasoned junior high English teacher as her worst student ever. One of our assignments was to keep a journal and write a couple of paragraphs in it at least five days a week. At the end of the quarter, we would turn in our journals for Mrs. Smith's review. She told us she wouldn't grade us on specific content, just whether we had completed the required number of entries. If there were entries that we didn't want her to read because they had sensitive or embarrassing material, she told us that we could dog-ear or paperclip the pages. She committed to not read that portion of our journals.

It should come as no surprise to you that I had some issues by the time I got to junior high school, and as a result, I had some sensitive journal entries. You will recall that a couple of years after I entered foster care, my birth mother passed away after her brief struggle with cancer. A few years after that, my biological father's parental rights were terminated.

By the time seventh grade came along, I was not doing

well in foster care. Life at home was difficult. My foster parents were good people, but I was one of eight children in their care. At times I clashed pretty severely with one or both of my foster parents. On more than one occasion, I physically lashed out at the other kids in the home. After one of these physical altercations, my foster dad sent me to my room to simmer down while he stood guard outside my door to make sure I stayed put. I responded by punching a hole through the door panel, and then escaping through the window and running away to a friend's home until everyone cooled down a bit.

School life was better—I had some really amazing teachers that year, and I got along with most of my classmates. English was something else though. Mrs. Smith and I didn't exactly see eye to eye. For my part, I was certainly disruptive from time to time—passing notes to girls around my seat near the back of the class or telling jokes about materials we were studying. I definitely wasn't great at raising my hand before making a comment.

She was pretty cruel in return. She would frequently single me out in class when we discussed class readings. If I hadn't done the readings, she would lecture me in class about the dangers of being lazy, and if I had done the readings, she would criticize my discussion of the material.

When I wrote in my journal as required, I didn't hold back. I was honest, I was specific, and I was brutal. On days when I had a particularly rough time in her class, I would record what I thought of my English teacher, generally using cruel, crude, and profane language—definitely TV-MA material by today's standards.

When it came time to turn in my journal, I was careful to paperclip the pages that included tirades against my English teacher. Just to be safe, I also paper-clipped any other pages that contained particularly profane content.

Two weeks into the second term, my English teacher returned our journals at the start of class. She called each student's name out, and we walked to the front of the class to pick up our journals so that we could continue the assignment during the second term. When she called my name, I walked to the front of the class and retrieved my journal. I turned around and started back to my desk.

I was about five steps away when she said, for the whole class to hear, "And Robert. I don't appreciate what you wrote about me in your journal."

I stopped, my face burning. The low chatter in the class that had been ongoing during the journal return process abruptly stopped. Several of my profanity-laced tirades in the journal flashed through my mind, and I realized with horror that she had read them all. Staring straight to the back of the class, avoiding any eye contact with my now-gawking classmates, I responded through gritted teeth, "You said you wouldn't read the paper-clipped pages."

"You clipped too many. I needed to make sure you were doing the assignment."

My temper began to rise. I turned around and glared at her, and with malice in my eyes and voice said, "You told us you wanted us to be honest, and I honestly think you're a bitch."

I don't remember the rest of the conversation, and I don't remember what the principal said shortly thereafter when I was sent to the office. I only remember my humiliation and shame.

So yeah, I wasn't a model student. Not in seventh grade, not in eighth grade, and not for most of ninth grade.

But, as I discussed in Chapter 2, a couple of years after the episode that earned me the title of Worst Student Ever, I discovered that I could be the master of my own fate, and I chose to be a better student. Virtually overnight, I began to get As instead of Cs and Ds.

There was no change in my ability, just a change in my choices. I chose to take the time to do my schoolwork. Instead of turning in assignments late, or not at all, I made sure that I turned in all of my assignments on time. If I didn't understand an assignment, or had questions after class, I chose to ask for help from teachers or aids. Once I actually did my homework, I started to understand the subject matter in my classes better, and once I started to understand the subject matter, I started to test better and get better grades.

If you would have asked my freshmen teachers what they thought my future would look like after the first three quarters of that year, they would likely have projected a fairly bleak outcome. By the time I graduated from high school, however, my grades were good enough to be admitted into some of the most prestigious public and private universities in the country.

I went to college and graduated with a Bachelor of Science in business management—finance, a field that had pretty good employment prospects. Even with the failed semester on my transcript discussed in Chapter 4, I was able to secure several excellent job offers in my field. But I knew that a four-year degree would not be the end of my education.

While we were on our honeymoon, my wife and I decided that after we graduated from college, I should get either a Master of Business Administration degree (a two-year program), or a Juris Doctor degree (a three-year program).

So, during my last semester of college, I took the entrance exams for both programs—the Graduate Management Admissions Test for business school and the Law School Admission Test for law school. I did well enough on both tests to apply to excellent business and law schools throughout the country. After I graduated and began working full time, my wife and I decided that I should apply to law school.

Once I was accepted to law school, I informed my employer that I would be leaving to continue my education later that Fall. He congratulated me but warned me that over the next several months, he would try to talk me out of leaving.

And try he did. Nothing he said or did tempted me to alter my course. I knew that the chances were that I would be able to earn more with a Juris Doctor degree than with just my undergraduate business degree alone.

About a week before my last scheduled day of work, my boss pulled me aside to make a final push to persuade me to keep working. He said, "Rob, you have a really bright future with our company. You are a fantastic employee, a rising star. I really think it would be a mistake for you to leave a great job for three more years of school."

I responded, as graciously as I could, "I really appreciate that. It's been excellent to work here, but my wife and I are quite unified in this decision."

In a last-ditch effort, he simply said, "Three years, Rob. Three years." I thought a bit about that. Three more years of school, and I knew that my law school strictly prohibited law students from having any sort of employment during the first year of study, so money was going to be tight.

Thankfully, my dad had already helped give me the proper perspective. He was a medical doctor—an eye sur-geon—who had attended four years of medical school after college, plus several years of residency training after that. As I was contemplating going to law school, he advised me, "Rob, no matter what you do, in three years you will be three years older. You can choose to be three years older as you are, or you can be three years older with a law degree you'll have for the rest of your life."

I left my job and went to law school. I worked hard, and when I graduated, I was fortunate to get a job with a prestigious law firm with offices across the United States and Europe. That three-year investment in myself immediately paid off: my starting salary was nearly a 300% increase over my salary at the job I had immediately before law school.

Law School graduation

After graduation, I continued to gain skills that I could use to make a living. I wanted to be a business trial lawyer, so I immediately sought tasks in my firm that would teach me how to excel in the courtroom and in conducting cases. I requested from the firm's partners any cases that were too small or insignificant to justify the hourly rate of more seasoned lawyers. In a relatively short period of time, they started giving me those cases and assignments, and I started attracting cases of my own.

Eventually, I started my own law firm, focused on what I had previously been trained to do well—complex business litigation. At first, my law firm was extremely successful, but an international recession slowed down international economies leading many of my clients to become unable to meet their financial obligations for my services. My revenues dried up, and my business failed. It was stressful, but because I had received a marketable degree, and I had marketable skills, I knew that I could get a job to support myself and my family.

My education and experience gave me options. I could choose to continue trying to make my business work. Or I could choose to go to work for a law firm or the legal department of a company. Or I could choose to change industries altogether and look to a new field where my education and skills would be applicable.

I discussed with my wife the different options my education and training afforded us. Together, we decided that I would continue operating my small law firm for a few more months to see if I could attract a sufficient number of clients who were able to pay their legal bills. Although those efforts were relatively successful, my wife and I ultimately decided that I would take my clients and join a larger firm. After making that decision, it took less than a week to find a large firm interested in having me join one of their offices.

This was made possible because of my choice to get as much education as I could. This isn't to say that a professional degree is for everyone. And please don't interpret my story as meaning that even a college degree is for everyone. But it is a clear example of the financial benefits of taking your education seriously. As noted before, if you are playing the averages, your earning potential generally goes up as your education goes up. And as your earning potential increases, so does your ability to avoid the stress, heartache, and anxiety that nearly always comes with not being able to meet your own financial needs.

You may be thinking, "I can't ever be a good student." My response is simple—why not? Remember Chapter 1? *Know that you can do it!* There was no way that a malnourished, undertrained six-year-old should have been able to finish a marathon. But he did, because that kid believed he could do it, and he didn't know that he couldn't.

Your education deserves your greatest efforts. Choose to become a good student, and you will be a good student. You don't have to be the very best in the class. You don't have to be anyone's star student. You just need to be *your* very best. I didn't set any speed records running the Honolulu Marathon as a six-year-old. I just finished it, and that was success.

I'm not going to tell you what subjects you should study or what field you should go into. You have interests, talents and skills that are unique to you. Focus on those, remembering that whatever you choose to study, you are looking for something that will provide skills and training that someone will pay you a living wage to do.

That said, one subject *everyone* should study is basic financial literacy. It will do you little good to have a well-paying job if you don't understand the basics of personal economics. Subjects of budgeting, saving, paying bills on time, and investing are of utmost importance if you want to avoid the pitfalls of poverty. You need to apply some of your mental power to learning and implementing that knowledge. No matter how much money you make, if you do not understand how to manage your money and expenses, you are setting yourself up for unnecessary pain and suffering. There are many highly trained professionals—including doctors and lawyers—who are stressed beyond words because they do not understand personal finance.

One of my favorite books on personal finance is *The Richest Man in Babylon* by George S. Clason. It is about the length of this book, and it teaches some very fundamental principles of personal finance through short parables. It tells a fictional story about a poor young man who became exceptionally wealthy in ancient Babylon through applying tried and true basic financial principals. The book was published nearly 100 years ago, yet the finance skills it teaches are timeless.

You might ask, "Rob, how am I ever going to pay for an advanced education?" If you have the desire to get a better education, you can find a way to pay for it. One of the few advantages of being a foster kid is that there are programs and scholarships available specifically because you were a ward of your state.

If you have a desire to get post-high school education, and you are willing to do the work for it, there will be a way to pay for it. Many states offer tuition waivers for kids who grew up in, or aged out of, foster care. In the digital age, Google is your friend. Search, and you will find options. At the end of this book is an appendix that lists various national and state resources you can use to jumpstart your search of assistance in financing your post high school education.

One avenue of financing education, which could simultaneously help you put the law of reciprocity to work in your favor, is to utilize various programs that exchange education financing for military service. I am not saying that path is for everyone, but it is a viable, and honorable option. Regardless of your political views, there is something noble about serving your country.

Of course, there is also the pure sweat method. While in college, I almost always had a job working 15-25 hours a week. That certainly cut into my social life, but it helped pay the bills. In my second and third years of law school, I worked full time in addition to attending school full time. That was incredibly taxing, but I decided that my education was worth it. I constantly told myself that I could do anything for two years, and my wife and I found a way to make it work, even with a young son born a few months before law school started.

I can promise you this: if you exercise your power to choose in favor of getting an education, your life path will change for the better forever. Make getting an education a preeminent priority in your life. Start now. If you are a subpar student, choose to do what you need to do to be a better student. Even if your last educational experience resulted in complete failure, try again. Do your work. You don't need to go it alone. Every school has resources to help you if you're struggling. Coming from the Worst Student Ever who failed an entire half-year of college, believe me when I say that you can succeed. Now go do it.

CONCLUSION

Thank you for sticking with me through these pages. There is something uplifting about finishing anything (Well, almost anything. I finished a 1.75-quart carton of Tillamook Utterly Chocolate Ice Cream while editing this book. I feel more weighed down than uplifted, but you get the point). You found a way to finish this book, and that's something!

In parting, remember that you are needed. Your example is needed to help others in our society see that they can overcome; they can do hard things. You can be that example and you can have a life full of deep and meaningful human connection.

I know you have what it takes to do it, but you need to know that you can do it too. If a six-year-old kid can finish a marathon, you can tackle whatever you want to. If anybody tells you that you can't, especially yourself, don't listen.

Your greatest tool is your ability to consciously choose. You can choose to not be a victim; to rise up; to not be alone; to serve others. You can choose success. Fiercely guard that ability to choose by staying away from anything that could lead to addictive or compulsive behaviors that deprive you of your freedom of choice, whether it's drugs, alcohol, pornography or any other mind or emotion-numbing substance.

You are not alone. There are others who can and will help you if you ask for that help. Even if you don't see anyone, choose to believe in the Divine, some higher power that knows you and is working for your good.

Put the law of reciprocity to work in your favor. Begin serving others and sending out goodness to the world, and you will stack the deck of life in your favor as that goodness is returned to you in amplified measure.

Focus on your education. Work to get the training and skills that will help you provide for yourself, and for those you love.

I'm like you, only 25 years in the future. Like you, I've experienced hurt, loneliness, abuse, rejection and abandonment. Years from now, I hope you can look back and see that you have found love, belonging, contentment, and acceptance notwithstanding your experience in foster care.

I wish you the very best in your efforts to rise above the difficulties and trauma that you've faced so early in your life. My deepest hope for you is that you know that you can have lasting and meaningful human connections, where you can love and be loved, where you can need and be needed. And I hope that, starting today, you go and make that your reality.

APPENDIX

This appendix contains certain resources that can assist you as you prepare to transition to adulthood. It is by not intended to be a comprehensive list of all resources you may need. Rather, this is merely a guide to point you in the right direction. Candidly, this appendix isn't even intended to be your first stop for information—you should be able to get more current and comprehensive information from your case worker, transition to adult living coordinator, or court-appointed special advocate. I would urge you to turn to them first for guidance finding educational, housing and healthcare resources. But in the event that you do not have ready access to those people, I hope that the information in the following pages can help you on your own personal road to success.

Putting together an appendix of services available to youth aging out of foster care is complicated by the fact that the United States is a democratic republic. Although a central, national government is essential for certain functions (say, national defense), state and local governments are more suited for understanding and meeting the social needs of its citizens. As a result, child welfare services, including services for foster youth, are largely provided on a state-by-state basis.

As a result, while some resources are available nationwide, most available assistance is state-specific. This appendix is organized accordingly. First, I have included certain national resources that are likely to be available to you regardless of where you lived as a foster child. Next, you will find, state by state, online resources in three areas—education financing; housing assistance; and mental and healthcare resources. Use these resources to launch your search for help.

Remember, you are not alone, but you have to exercise your power to choose to access the help you need. If you hit a roadblock, keep going until you find what you are looking for. You can do it. Good luck, my friend.

NATIONAL

➤ GENERAL:

U.S. Department of Education Foster Care Transition Toolkit: https://www2.ed.gov/about/inits/ed/foster-care/youth-transition-toolkit.pdf

Foster Club National Resources: https://www.fosterclub.com/resources

➤ EDUCATION:

Federal Student Aid: https://studentaid.gov

State by state tuition waivers: https://depts.washington.edu/fostered/tuition-waivers-state

College scholarships for foster kids: http://www.collegescholarships.org/scholarships/foster.htm

Foster Care To Success: https://www.fc2success.org/programs/scholarships-and-grants/

College Rank – Helping foster kids pay for college: https://www.collegerank.net/helping-foster-kids-pay-for-college/

Fastweb – Connection to scholarships and financial aid: https://www.fastweb.com

Affordable College – From Foster Care to College: https://www.affordablecolleges online.org/college-resource-center/foster-care-to-college/

Scholarships.com: https://scholarships.com

Military service education information: https://www.todaysmilitary.com/education-training/paying-college

➤ HOUSING:

HUD – Foster Youth to Independence information: https://www.hud.gov/press/press_releases_media_advisories/HUD_No_19_111

https://www.hud.gov/program_offices/public_indian_housing/programs/hcv/fyi_tpv

John H. Chafee Foster Care Program Information: https://fas.org/sgp/crs/misc/IF11070.pdf

➤ MEDICAL:

General Medicaid and CHIP information: https://www.medicaid.gov/state-resource-center/mac-learning-collaboratives/downloads/foster-care-ensuring-access.pdf

Health Care for Former Foster Youth: https://www.fosterclub.com/healthcareffy

ALABAMA

➤ **EDUCATION:**

Foster Care To Success: https://www.fc2sprograms.org/alabama-fostering-hope-scholarship/; https://www.fc2sprograms.org/alabama/

Fostering Hope Scholarship: https://dhr.alabama.gov/wp-content/uploads/2020/02/Alabama-Fostering-Hope-Flyer.pdf

➤ **HOUSING:**

Independent Living Program General Information: https://dhr.alabama.gov/foster-care/independent-living-program/

➤ **MEDICAL:**

Medicaid Application: https://medicaid.alabama.gov/content/3.0_Apply/

ALASKA

➤ **EDUCATION:**

Alaska DHS Financial Assistance for Post-Secondary Education and Training: http://dhss.alaska.gov/ocs/Pages/independentliving/etv.aspx

➤ **HOUSING:**

Alaska Housing Finance Corporation: https://www.ahfc.us/publichousing/rental-programs/low-income-alaskans-parole-or-probation-youth-aging-out-foster-care

Independent Living Program Coordinators: http://dhss.alaska.gov/ocs/Pages/independentliving/contact.aspx

➤ **MEDICAL:**

Medicaid to 26: Alaska: https://jlc.org/medicaid-26-alaska

ARIZONA

> **EDUCATION:**

Foster Care to Success: https://www.fc2sprograms.org/arizona/

> **HOUSING:**

Arizona Young Adult Program: https://dcs.az.gov/services/young-adult/young-adult-program

> **MEDICAL:**

Young Adult Transitional Insurance: http://www.fosteringadvocatesarizona.org/young-adult-transitional-insurance-yati/

ARKANSAS

> **EDUCATION:**

Arkansas Education and Training Voucher (ETV) Program: (501) 682-2447; https://humanservices.arkansas.gov/about-dhs/dcfs/programs-services

> **HOUSING:**

Micah's House NWA: http://www.micahshousenwa.org

Immerse Arkansas: https://immersearkansas.org; (501) 404-9890

Saving Grace NWA: https://www.savinggracenwa.org/housing

Second Chance Youth Ranch: https://www.2cyr.org

> **MEDICAL:**

FosterClub Arkansas: 503-717-1552; outreach@fosterclub.com

CALIFORNIA

➤ EDUCATION:

Financial Aid Guide for California Foster Youth: http://www.jbaforyouth.org/wp-content/uploads/2018/01/Financial-aid-guide-final-Jan-18.pdf

California Chafee Grant for Foster Youth: https://chafee.csac.ca.gov

➤ HOUSING:

John Burton Advocates for Youth – THP-Plus: http://www.jbaforyouth.org/thp/

➤ MEDICAL:

DHCS FFY Program: https://www.dhcs.ca.gov/services/medi-cal/eligibility/Pages/FFY.aspx

COLORADO

➤ EDUCATION:

Colorado Dept. of Education: https://www.cde.state.co.us/dropoutprevention/fsfostercareandhighereducation

The Denver Foundation Scholarships: http://www.denverfoundation.org/Scholarships/Scholarships-at-the-Denver-Foundation

➤ HOUSING:

Homeless Solutions Program: https://cdola.colorado.gov/homeless-solutions-program-project-based-vouchers-request-applications

Urban Peak: https://www.urbanpeak.org

➤ MEDICAL:

Health First Colorado: https://www.healthfirstcolorado.com

Health First Colorado Former Foster Care Youth FAQ: https://www.colorado.gov/pacific/hcpf/member-faqs; (800) 221-3943

CONNECTICUT

➤ **EDUCATION:**

FosterClub Connecticut: (503) 717-1552; outreach@fosterclub.com

➤ **HOUSING:**

Community Housing Assistance Program: http://www.crtct.org/en/need-help/
housing-a-shelters/chap; (860) 895-6634; CHAP@crtct.org

➤ **MEDICAL:**

DCF Health Advocate Unit: https://portal.ct.gov/DCF/Health-and-Wellness/Health-
Advocates/Home

DELAWARE

➤ **EDUCATION:**

Delaware DSCYF Independent Living: https://kids.delaware.gov/fs/independent-living
.shtml

➤ **HOUSING:**

Dunamis: https://www.dunamishodi.org

West End Neighborhood House: http://www.westendnh.org/youth-families/services-
for-foster-care-youth/

➤ **MEDICAL:**

Delaware Assist: https://assist.dhss.delaware.gov

DISTRICT OF COLUMBIA

➤ **EDUCATION:**

Foster Care To Success: https://www.fc2sprograms.org/washington-d-c/

➤ **HOUSING:**

Rapid Housing Assistance Program: https://cfsa.dc.gov/sites/default/files/dc/sites/
cfsa/publication/attachments/AI%20-%20Rapid%20Housing%20Assistance%20
Program%20%28RHAP%29%20%28final%29_3.pdf

➤ **MEDICAL:**

Department of Health Care Finance: https://dhcf.dc.gov/service/former-foster-
care-youth

FLORIDA

➤ **EDUCATION:**

Florida DCF Tuition Fee Exemption: https://www.myflfamilies.com/service-programs/
independent-living/tuition-fee-exemption.shtml

➤ **HOUSING:**

Daniel Postsecondary Educational Support Services: https://www.danielkids.org/
our-programs/floridas-i-l-resource-center/

ImPower – The Village: https://www.impowerfl.org/what-we-do/the-village/

➤ **MEDICAL:**

Florida DCF Access Florida: https://www.myflorida.com/accessflorida/

GEORGIA

➤ EDUCATION:

Georgia ETV: https://embarkgeorgia.org/etv/

Georgia ETV Webinar: https://www.youtube.com/watch?v=YJ48fQSFaPs&feature=youtu.be

➤ HOUSING:

Wellroot Transitional and Independent Living: https://wellroot.org/our-programs/tlp-ilp/

GA/RYSE: https://www.garyse-ilp.org/programs/housing-support

➤ MEDICAL:

Georgia Gateway Application: https://gateway.ga.gov/access/accessController?id=a56d2ab36e6a0814887af9b44%20%20&id=a56d2ab36e6a0814887af9b44%20%20_

HAWAII

➤ EDUCATION:

Hawaii DHS Higher Education Stipend: https://shakatown.com/youth/education?page=financial_help

➤ HOUSING:

Hawaii DHS Independent Living Program: https://humanservices.hawaii.gov/ssd/home/child-welfare-services/ilp/

Hale Kipa: https://www.halekipa.org/yfc/; (808) 589-1829, ext. 233

➤ MEDICAL:

PoweredTil26: http://www.poweredtil26.org

Medicaid Application: (877) 628-5076; www.mybenefits.hawaii.gov

IDAHO

➤ **EDUCATION:**

Idaho ETV Program: https://healthandwelfare.idaho.gov/Portals/0/Children/
AdoptionFoster/ETVDescription.pdf

➤ **HOUSING:**

JEM Friends: http://www.jemfriends.org/housing/

➤ **MEDICAL:**

Idaho DHW Medicaid Program: https://healthandwelfare.idaho.gov/medical/medicaid/
tabid/123/default.aspx

ILLINOIS

➤ **EDUCATION:**

Foster Progress Financial Aid Logic Tree: http://www.foster-progress.org/financial-aid

Illinois ETV Program Information: https://www2.illinois.gov/dcfs/aboutus/notices/
documents/cfs_449-3_application_for_education_and_training_voucher_funds_
(fillable).pdf

➤ **HOUSING:**

Cook County Public Guardian Youth Housing Assistance Program: (312) 814-5571;
https://www.publicguardian.org/juvenile/youth-resources/housing/

➤ **MEDICAL:**

Application for Benefits Eligibility: (800) 843-6154; https://abe.illinois.gov/abe/
access/

INDIANA

➤ **EDUCATION:**

Indiana ETV Application: https://indianaetv.org

➤ **HOUSING:**

Indiana Housing Programs for Youth Aging Out: https://www.in.gov/dcs/2408.htm

➤ **MEDICAL:**

Indiana FSSA Benefits Portal: https://fssabenefits.in.gov/bp/#/

IOWA

➤ **EDUCATION:**

Iowa ETV: https://www.iowacollegeaid.gov/ETV

All Iowa Opportunity Scholarship: https://www.iowacollegeaid.gov/AllIowaOpportunityScholarship

➤ **HOUSING:**

Iowa Aftercare Services Network: https://www.yss.org/program/iowa-aftercare-services-network/; https://www.iowaaftercare.org/Resources/Housing%20Resources.html; https://www.iowafinance.com/aftercare-rent-subsidy-program/

➤ **MEDICAL:**

Iowa DHS Services Portal: https://dhsservices.iowa.gov/apspssp/ssp.portal

KANSAS

➤ EDUCATION:

Kansas Tuition and Fee Waiver: https://registrar.ku.edu/kansas-foster-child-education-assistance-act

Application for Foster Child Education Assistance Program: http://www.dcf.ks.gov/services/PPS/Documents/PPM_Forms/Section_7000_Forms/PPS7260.pdf

Kansas ETV: http://www.dcf.ks.gov/services/PPS/Pages/Education-and-Training-Voucher.aspx

ETV Form: http://www.dcf.ks.gov/services/PPS/Documents/PPM_Forms/Section_7000_Forms/PPS7001.pdf

➤ HOUSING:

Kansas DCF Independent Living Program: http://www.dcf.ks.gov/services/pps/pages/independentlivingprogram.aspx

Lawrence-Douglas Housing Authority Next Step Vouchers: (785) 842-8110; https://storage.googleapis.com/wzukusers/user-31752601/documents/5b23167be55a8pfdgjxF/Next%20Step%20Program.pdf

➤ MEDICAL:

Kansas DHCF Health Benefits Program: https://www.kdheks.gov/hcf/medical_assistance/eligibility.html; http://www.dcf.ks.gov/services/PPS/Pages/Aged-Out-Medical-Program.aspx

KENTUCKY

➤ **EDUCATION:**

Kentucky Higher Education Assistance Authority: https://www.kheaa.com/website/ kheaa/kheaaprograms?main=1

Kentucky ETV: chafee.ilp@ky.gov

KY Rise: https://prdweb.chfs.ky.gov/kyrise/Home/Education

➤ **HOUSING:**

KY Rise Aftercare Services: https://prdweb.chfs.ky.gov/kyrise/Home/AftercareServices

➤ **MEDICAL:**

Kentucky Medicaid: https://benefind.ky.gov

LOUISIANA

➤ **EDUCATION:**

Louisiana Office of Student Financial Assistance: https://mylosfa.la.gov/ students-parents/scholarships-grants/chafee/

➤ **MEDICAL:**

Louisiana Health Coverage Application: (888) 342-6207; http://ldh.la.gov/index.cfm/ page/237.

Louisiana Medicaid Information Sheet: http://ldh.la.gov/assets/medicaid/ MedicaidEligibilityForms/FosterCareYouthFlyerEng.pdf

MAINE

➤ **EDUCATION:**

Finance Authority of Maine Tuition Waiver Program: https://www.famemaine.com/
maine_grants_loans/tuition-waiver-program/

➤ **HOUSING:**

Chaffee Foster Care Independence Program: https://www.maine.gov/dhhs/ocfs/cw/
chafee.htm

➤ **MEDICAL:**

My Maine Connection: (855) 797-4357; https://www1.maine.gov/benefits/account/
login.html

MARYLAND

➤ **EDUCATION:**

Maryland Youth Launching Initiatives For Empowerment: https://mdconnectmylife.
mymdthink.maryland.gov/resources/education/

Maryland Tuition Waiver for Foster Care Recipients: https://mhec.maryland.gov/
preparing/Pages/FinancialAid/ProgramDescriptions/prog_fostercare.aspx

➤ **HOUSING:**

City Steps: https://airseffect.org/youth-supportive-housing-1

Maryland Independent Living Services: https://dhs.maryland.gov/foster-care/
youth-resources/independent-living/

➤ **MEDICAL:**

Maryland Health Connection: (855) 642-8573; https://mmcp.health.maryland.gov/
Pages/Former-Foster-Care-Youth.aspx

MASSACHUSETTS

➤ **EDUCATION:**

DCF Foster Child Tuition Waiver and Fee Assistance: https://www.mass.edu/osfa/programs/dcffoster.asp

Adolescent Tuition Assistance: https://www.mass.gov/service-details/adolescent-tuition-assistance

Massachusetts Education Financing Authority: https://www.mefa.org

➤ **HOUSING:**

The Answer Book: https://www.mass.gov/info-details/the-answer-book-housing-after-i-leave-foster-care

➤ **MEDICAL:**

Massachusetts Health Connector: https://www.mahealthconnector.org

MICHIGAN

➤ **EDUCATION:**

Fostering Futures Scholarship: https://www.michigan.gov/setwithmet/0,4666,7-374-87551_61346-331411--,00.html

Michigan ETV: https://www.michigan.gov/fyit/0,1607,7-240-44289-160381--,00.html; https://mietv.samaritas.org

Supportive Programming/Scholarships for Foster Youth: https://www.fcnp.org/resources-2/education/

➤ **HOUSING:**

Foster Youth in Transition: https://www.michigan.gov/fyit/0,4585,7-240-44293---,00.html

Fostering Success Michigan: http://fosteringsuccessmichigan.com/library/life-domain/housing

➤ **MEDICAL:**

Transitional Medicaid: https://www.michigan.gov/documents/fyit/FAQ_FosterCare_Transitional_Medicaid_338956_7.pdf

MI Bridges Application for Benefits: https://newmibridges.michigan.gov/s/isd-landing-page?language=en_US

MINNESOTA

➤ EDUCATION:

Minnesota ETV: https://mn.gov/dhs/people-we-serve/children-and-families/services/ adolescent-services/programs-services/education-and-training-voucher.jsp

Minnesota Office of Higher Education: https://www.ohe.state.mn.us/mPg.cfm? PageID=1385

➤ HOUSING:

Family Unification Program: https://mn.hb101.org/a/17/

➤ MEDICAL:

MNSure Application: https://www.mnsure.org

MISSISSIPPI

➤ EDUCATION:

Education Training Voucher: Contact your Independent Living Coordinator: (601) 359-4572; (601) 359-4874; (601) 954-5590

➤ HOUSING:

Contact your Independent Living Coordinator: (601) 359-4572; (601) 359-4874; (601) 954-5590

➤ MEDICAL:

Mississippi Medicaid: (800) 421-2408; https://medicaid.ms.gov/medicaid-coverage/ how-to-apply/

MISSOURI

➤ EDUCATION:

Missouri Reach: https://dss.mo.gov/cd/older-youth-program/files/missouri-reach-brochure.pdf; mo@statevoucher.org

Missouri ETV: https://dss.mo.gov/cd/older-youth-program/education.htm

Missouri Tuition and Fee Waiver: http://revisor.mo.gov/main/OneSection.aspx?section=173.270&bid=8815&hl=

Foster Care to Success: https://www.fc2sprograms.org/missouri/

Missouri Credential Completion & Employment: https://www.fc2sprograms.org/mo-reach-credential-completion-and-employment-program/

➤ HOUSING:

DSS Older Youth Program: https://dss.mo.gov/cd/older-youth-program/; https://dss.mo.gov/cd/older-youth-program/transitional-living-program.htm

DSS Aftercare Services: https://dss.mo.gov/cd/older-youth-program/aftercare.htm

Epworth Independent Living Program: https://www.epworth.org/programs/independent-living-program-ilp/

Youth in Need: https://www.youthinneed.org/RESOURCES/Housing

➤ MEDICAL:

Missouri HealthNet Coverage: https://dss.mo.gov/cd/older-youth-program/files/free-health-insurance-former-foster-care-youth.pdf

MONTANA

➤ **EDUCATION:**

Montana Foster Care: Scholarships and Financial Aid: http://opi.mt.gov/Leadership/
Academic-Success/Title-Other-Federal-Programs/Neglected-Delinquent-or-At-Risk-
Youth/Foster-Care/Foster-Care-Scholarships-and-Financial-Aid

Reach Higher Montana: https://www.reachhighermontana.org/we-can-help/youth-in-
foster-care

Dawson Promise: https://www.dawson.edu/outreach/dawson-promise.html
(also includes housing)

➤ **HOUSING:**

Montana Chafee Foster Care Independence Program: https://dphhs.mt.gov/CFSD/
FosterCareIndependence.aspx

➤ **MEDICAL:**

Montana Medicaid: https://apply.mt.gov/; (888) 706-1535

NEBRASKA

➤ **EDUCATION:**

Nebraska ETV Program: http://www.central-plains.org/etv.html

Project Everlast Scholarships: https://www.projecteverlast.org/related/resources.html

Lincoln Community Foundation: https://www.lcf.org/impacting-community/student-
scholarships

➤ **HOUSING:**

DHHS Bridge to Independence: (402) 314-8294; http://dhhs.ne.gov/Pages/Bridge-to-
Independence.aspx

Project Everlast Opportunity Passport: https://www.fhasinc.org/opportunity-passport.html

Project Everlast Transitional Services: https://www.projecteverlast.org/lincoln/transitional.
html

➤ **MEDICAL:**

Nebraska Appleseed: https://neappleseed.org/coveredtil26NE

Medicaid Application: www.AccessNebraska.ne.gov

NEVADA

➤ EDUCATION:

Nevada Foster Youth Financial Aid Toolkit (including tuition waiver): https://nshe.nevada.edu/initiatives/foster-youth/foster-youth-financial-aid/

The Children's Cabinet ETV: https://www.childrenscabinet.org/family-youth/youth-education-and-training/foster-youth-support

Children's Advocacy Alliance: https://www.caanv.org/see-what-we-are-doing/foster-youth-scholarships-and-grants/

➤ HOUSING:

Nevada Independent Living Program: http://dcfs.nv.gov/Programs/CWS/IL/

➤ MEDICAL:

Nevada Aged Out Medicaid Insurance: http://dcfs.nv.gov/uploadedFiles/dcfsnvgov/content/Programs/CWS/IL/AgedOutMedicaidAppforWebsiteRev2017.pdf

NEW HAMPSHIRE

➤ EDUCATION:

New Hampshire Aftercare Services: https://www.dhhs.nh.gov/dcyf/aftercare.htm

DHHS Adolescent Program: https://www.dhhs.nh.gov/dcyf/adolescent.htm

New Hampshire Higher Education Assistance Foundation: https://www.nhheaf.org/star-program.asp

➤ HOUSING:

New Hampshire Family Unification Program: https://www.nhhfa.org/rental-assistance/housing-choice-voucher-program/special-programs/

DHHS Housing Resources: https://www.dhhs.nh.gov/dcyf/housing.htm

Manchester Housing and Redevelopment Authority:

➤ MEDICAL:

DHHS Medicaid Notice: https://www.dhhs.nh.gov/dcyf/documents/medicaid-for-former-fc.pdf

New Hampshire Medicaid Application: https://nheasy.nh.gov

NEW JERSEY

➤ **EDUCATION:**

New Jersey Youth Resource Spot: https://www.nj.gov/njyrs/resources/

New Jersey Foster Care Scholars Program (including tuition waiver):
https://www.embrella.org/pdf/scholarship/resources.pdf
https://www.embrella.org/pdf/scholarship/njfc-overview.pdf

Higher Education Student Assistance Authority: https://www.hesaa.org/Pages/default.aspx

➤ **HOUSING:**

New Jersey Youth Resource Spot: https://www.nj.gov/njyrs/

➤ **MEDICAL:**

Medicaid Extension for Young Adults: (888) 235-4766

NJ Family Care: http://www.njfamilycare.org/default.aspx

NEW MEXICO

➤ **EDUCATION:**

New Mexico CFYD Educational Support: https://cyfd.org/terrific-teens/educational-support#

New Mexico Tuition Waiver: https://albuquerquefoundation.org/uploads/files/Tuition-WaiverLaw(2).pdf

Albuquerque Community Foundation Youth in Foster Care Scholarship: https://albuquerquefoundation.org/youth-in-foster-care-scholarship-program.aspx

New Mexico Friends of Foster Children: http://www.nmffc.org/applications/; http://www.nmffc.org/wp-content/uploads/2020/05/NMFFCApplication2020.pdf

➤ **HOUSING:**

New Mexico CFYD Transitions: https://cyfd.org/transition-services/permanent-supportive-housing-for-cyfd-involved-youth

➤ **MEDICAL:**

New Mexico Medicaid Application: (855) 637-6574; https://www.hsd.state.nm.us/LookingForAssistance/apply-for-benefits.aspx

NEW YORK

> ## EDUCATION:

New York ETV Program Application: https://etv-nys.smapply.org

Foster Youth College Success Initiative: http://www.nysed.gov/postsecondary-services/foster-youth-college-success-initiative

The Excelsior Scholarship: https://www.ny.gov/programs/tuition-free-degree-program-excelsior-scholarship

New York OYD Scholarship Opportunities and College Resources: https://ocfs.ny.gov/main/youth/scholarly_resources.asp

Fostering Youth Success Alliance: https://www.fysany.org/college-success-guide

> ## HOUSING:

Housing Resources for Youth Aging Out of Foster Care: https://www.fysany.org/college-success-guide/chapter-5/housing-resources-youth-aging-out-foster-care

Supportive Housing Network of New York: https://shnny.org/supportive-housing/what-is-supportive-housing/youth-programs/ny-ny-iii-housing/

NYC Children Housing: https://www1.nyc.gov/site/acs/youth/housing.page

Generation NYC: https://growingupnyc.cityofnewyork.us/generationnyc/topics/foster-youth/

> ## MEDICAL:

Health Services for Children in Foster Care: https://ocfs.ny.gov/main/sppd/health-services/affordable-care-act.php

NORTH CAROLINA

➤ EDUCATION:

Foster Care to Success NC Reach: https://www.fc2sprograms.org/nc-reach/

North Carolina Reach Resources: https://www.ncreach.org/resources/

College Foundation of North Carolina: https://www.cfnc.org/apply/applyfinancialaid.jsp

➤ HOUSING:

Independent Living Services for Foster Children: https://www.ncdhhs.gov/assistance/state-guardianship/independent-living-services-for-foster-children

LINKS Program: http://www.wakegov.com/humanservices/children/links/Pages/default.aspx

➤ MEDICAL:

North Carolina Medicaid Application: https://medicaid.ncdhhs.gov/beneficiaries/get-started/apply-medicaid-or-health-choice

NORTH DAKOTA

➤ EDUCATION:

Chafee Foster Care Transition Program and ETV: (701) 328-4934; https://www.nd.gov/dhs/services/childfamily/fostercare/chafee.html

➤ HOUSING:

Chafee Independent Living Program: (701) 328-4934; https://www.nd.gov/dhs/info/pubs/docs/cfs/brochure-chafee-independent-living-program.pdf

➤ MEDICAL:

North Dakota Medicaid Coverage Former Foster Youth: https://www.nd.gov/dhs/info/pubs/docs/cfs/handout-medicaid-coverage-former-foster-youth.pdf

https://www.nd.gov/dhs/eligibility/

OHIO

➤ EDUCATION:

Ohio Foster Care To Success: https://www.fc2sprograms.org/ohio/

Ohio Department of Higher Education: https://www.ohiohighered.org/students/
prepare-for-college/foster-care-youth

Ohio Department of Education – Foster Care: http://education.ohio.gov/Topics/
Student-Supports/Foster-Care

Bridges: https://bridgestosuccess.jfs.ohio.gov/index.stm

➤ HOUSING:

Bridges: https://bridgestosuccess.jfs.ohio.gov/index.stm

Action Ohio Resource List: https://fosteractionohio.files.wordpress.com/
2019/01/2019-central-oh-resource-list-for-foster-youth.pdf

➤ MEDICAL:

Ohio Benefits: https://benefits.ohio.gov

OKLAHOMA

➤ **GENERAL:**

Oklahoma Successful Adulthood Program: https://oksa.ou.edu

➤ **EDUCATION:**

Oklahoma ETV: https://oksa.ou.edu/content/education-and-training-voucher-etv

Oklahoma DHS Tuition Waiver: https://bigfuture.collegeboard.org/scholarships
/independent-living-act-departmentof-human-services-tuition-waiver;
https://www.okhighered.org

Oklahoma College Scholarships: http://www.collegescholarships.org/states/oklahoma.htm

➤ **HOUSING:**

OKSA Housing Resources: https://oksa.ou.edu/resources/Housing

➤ **MEDICAL:**

SoonerCare Application: (800) 987-7767; http://www.okhca.org/individuals.aspx?id=11698

HealthPocket SoonerCare: https://www.healthpocket.com/medicaid-public-plans/plan/
soonercare-z2g84#.XwCN2C2z1UM

OREGON

➤ **EDUCATION:**

Oregon DSH Financial Aid for Higher Education: https://www.oregon.gov/DHS/
CHILDREN/FOSTERCARE/ILP/Pages/financial-aid.aspx

Oregon Chafee Education and Training Grant: https://oregonstudentaid.gov/
chafee-etg.aspx

➤ **HOUSING:**

Oregon DSH Independent Living Program: https://www.oregon.gov/DHS/CHILDREN/
FOSTERCARE/ILP/Pages/index.aspx

Family Unification Program and Foster Youth to Independence Housing Vouchers:
(503) 945-5684; ILP.Central@state.or.us

➤ **MEDICAL:**

Oregon Health Plan Application: https://www.oregon.gov/oha/HSD/OHP/Pages/apply.aspx

PENNSYLVANIA

➤ EDUCATION:

Pennsylvania Chafee Education and Training Grant Program: https://www.pheaa.org/funding-opportunities/other-educational-aid/chafee-program.shtml

Fostering Independence Tuition Waiver Program: https://www.education.pa.gov/Postsecondary-Adult/CollegeCareer/FosteringIndependence/Pages/default.aspx

➤ HOUSING:

Chafee Foster Care Independence Program: https://www.dhs.pa.gov/providers/Providers/Pages/Chafee-Foster-Care.aspx

Family Care for Children & Youth: https://www.fccy.org/independent-living/

Valley Youth House: https://www.valleyyouthhouse.org/programs/life-skills-development/independent-living-program/

Family Services of NWPA Independent Living Program: http://www.fsnwpa.org/our-services/parent-education/independent-living-program/

➤ MEDICAL:

HealthChoices Former Foster Youth: http://www.healthchoices.pa.gov/info/resources/former-foster-youth/index.htm

RHODE ISLAND

➤ EDUCATION:

DCYF Post-Secondary Tuition Assistance Program: http://www.dcyf.ri.gov/documents/DCYF-Postsecondary-Tuition-Assistance-Program-FAQs-2019-2020-Grant-Year.pdf

Higher Education Opportunity Incentive Grant Program Policy: http://www.dcyf.ri.gov/policyregs/higher_education_opportunity_incentive_grant_program_policy.htm

➤ HOUSING:

The Bridge Family Center Independent Living Programs: http://www.bridgefamilycenter.org/how-we-help/residential-services/independent-living/

➤ MEDICAL:

Health Source RI: https://healthyrhode.ri.gov/HIXWebI3/DisplayRIServices

SOUTH CAROLINA

➤ **EDUCATION:**

Department of Social Services Chafee/ETV Program: https://dss.sc.gov/foster-care/chafeeetv-program/

Commission on Higher Education Need-Based Grant Program: https://www.che.sc.gov/Students,FamiliesMilitary/PayingForCollege/FinancialAssistanceAvailable/ScholarshipsGrantsforSCResidents/SCNeed-basedGrantProgram.aspx

➤ **HOUSING:**

SCNYTD Transition Housing and Assistance: https://www.nytdstayconnected.com/newsroom/transition-housing-and-assistance/

➤ **MEDICAL:**

South Carolina Healthy Connections Former Foster Care: https://www.scdhhs.gov/eligibility-groups/former-foster-care-age-26

SOUTH DAKOTA

➤ **EDUCATION:**

Department of Social Services ETV Funds: https://dss.sd.gov/childprotection/independentlivingprogram/educationtraining.aspx

➤ **HOUSING:**

Department of Social Services Independent Living Program: https://dss.sd.gov/childprotection/independentlivingprogram/

➤ **MEDICAL:**

South Dakota Medicaid: https://dss.sd.gov/medicaid/generalinfo/medicalprograms.aspx#foster

Children's Home Society: https://chssd.org/prevention/resources/aces

TENNESSEE

➤ **EDUCATION:**

Tennessee HOPE Foster Child Tuition Grant: https://www.tn.gov/collegepays/
money-for-college/grant-programs/tn-hope-foster-child-tuition-grant.html

➤ **HOUSING:**

Department of Children's Services Independent Living: https://www.tn.gov/dcs/
program-areas/youth-in-transition/il.html

➤ **MEDICAL:**

TennCare Connection Application: https://tenncareconnect.tn.gov/services/homepage

TennCare Medicaid Policy: https://www.tn.gov/content/dam/tn/tenncare/documents/
FormerFosterCareChildrenUpToAge26.pdf

Youth Villages: https://www.youthvillages.org/services/lifeset/

TEXAS

➤ **EDUCATION:**

Texas Foster Youth Justice Project: http://texasfosteryouth.org/legal-resources/
legal-resources-for-youth/education/

Texas Education and Training Voucher Program: https://discoverbcfs.net/texasetv/

College for All Texans: http://www.collegeforalltexans.com/apps/financialaid/
tofa2.cfm?ID=480

➤ **HOUSING:**

Texas Foster Youth Justice Project: http://texasfosteryouth.org/legal-resources/
legal-resources-for-youth/housing/

Texas Youth Connection: https://www.dfps.state.tx.us/txyouth/housing/housing.asp

Department of Family and Protective Services Transitional Living Services: https://
www.dfps.state.tx.us/Child_Protection/Youth_and_Young_Adults/Transitional_
Living/default.asp

➤ **MEDICAL:**

Department of Family and Protective Services Medical Benefits: https://www.
dfps.state.tx.us/Child_Protection/Youth_and_Young_Adults/Transitional_Living/
medical_benefits.asp

UTAH

➤ **EDUCATION:**

Department of Human Services Education & Employment: https://dcfs.utah.gov/
services/youth-services/educationemployment/

WIOA Youth Program: https://jobs.utah.gov/wioa/07_145.pdf

Olene S. Walker Transition to Adult Living Scholarship: https://dcfs.utah.gov/
wp-content/uploads/2018/08/Things-to-know-before-you-apply-for-the-TAL-
Scholarship.pdf

➤ **HOUSING:**

Housing Authority Contacts: https://www.hud.gov/sites/dfiles/PIH/documents/
PHA_Contact_Report_UT.pdf

➤ **MEDICAL:**

Department of Human Services Health & Wellness: https://dcfs.utah.gov/services/
youth-services/health-wellness/

Apply for Medicaid: https://medicaid.utah.gov/apply-medicaid/

VERMONT

➤ **EDUCATION:**

Vermont Student Assistance Corporation Foster Care Scholarships:
https://www.vsac.org/pay/student-aid-options/scholarships/foster-care-youth

➤ **HOUSING:**

Youth Development Program: https://vtyouthdevelopmentprogram.org

Spectrum Youth & Family Services: http://www.spectrumvt.org/what-we-do/
supportive-housing/

HUD Family Unification Program: https://dcf.vermont.gov/oeo/fup

➤ **MEDICAL:**

Health Connect: (855) 899-9600; https://portal.healthconnect.vermont.gov/
VTHBELand/welcome.action

VIRGINIA

➤ **EDUCATION:**

Great Expectations: http://greatexpectations.vccs.edu

Education and Training Voucher Program: https://www.dss.virginia.gov/family/fc/etv.cgi

➤ **HOUSING:**

Fostering Futures: https://www.dss.virginia.gov/fmf/support.html

Project Life: https://www.vaprojectlife.org/for-young-adults/housing/

➤ **MEDICAL:**

Cover Virginia Application: (855) 242-8282; https://coverva.org/apply/

WASHINGTON

➤ **EDUCATION:**

Ready Set Grad Financial Aid: https://readysetgrad.wa.gov/filing-financial-aid-foster-youth

Department of Children, Youth & Families Education for Foster Youth: https://www.dcyf.wa.gov/services/education-for-foster-youth/etv

➤ **HOUSING:**

Independent Youth Housing Program: http://independence.wa.gov/programs/independent-youth-housing-program/

Department of Children, Youth & Families Education for Extended Foster Care: https://www.dcyf.wa.gov/services/extended-foster-care

Transitional Living Program: https://www.dcyf.wa.gov/services/independent-living-skills/transitional-living-program

➤ **MEDICAL:**

Apple Health Core Connections: (844) 354-9876; https://www.coordinatedcarehealth.com/members/foster-care.html

WEST VIRGINIA

➤ **EDUCATION:**

It's My Move Foster Care Education Opportunities: http://www.itsmymove.org/MyFuture.php

College Foundation of West Virginia: https://secure.cfwv.com/Financial_Aid_Planning/_default.aspx

West Virginia University Tuition Waiver: https://financialaid.wvu.edu/waivers/foster-care; http://modify.cedwvu.org/foster-care-tuition-waiver/

➤ **HOUSING:**

MODIFY: http://modify.cedwvu.org/services-and-eligibility/#main-content

It's My Move Transition Choices: https://www.itsmymove.org/choices.php

➤ **MEDICAL:**

Bureau for Children and Families Application and Eligibility: https://dhhr.wv.gov/bcf/Services/familyassistance/Pages/Medicaid.aspx

Medicaid Application: https://dhhr.wv.gov/bms/Members/Apply/Pages/default.aspx

WISCONSIN

➤ **EDUCATION:**

Youth Services Paying for College: https://dcf.wisconsin.gov/youthservices/college

Foster Care & Adoption Scholarship Information: https://wifostercareandadoption.org/resources/for-youth-in-care/scholarship-information/

➤ **HOUSING:**

Department of Children and Families Independent Living: https://dcf.wisconsin.gov/independentliving

➤ **MEDICAL:**

ACCESS: (800) 362-3002; https://access.wisconsin.gov/access/

WYOMING

➤ **EDUCATION:**

Department of Family Services Education and Training Vouchers: https://dfs.wyo.gov/services/child-youth-services/foster-care-foster-care-training/education-and-training-vouchers-etv/

➤ **HOUSING:**

Department of Family Services Independent Living Program: https://dfs.wyo.gov/services/child-youth-services/foster-care-foster-care-training/independent-living-program/

➤ **MEDICAL:**

Wyoming Medicaid Application: https://health.wyo.gov/healthcarefin/medicaid/programs-and-eligibility/

Notes

Notes

Notes

Notes

Notes

Notes

Notes

Made in the USA
Monee, IL
27 July 2020

37077651R00089